An A - Z for Lightworkers

by

Sheila C

D1437724

authors
On Line

Visit us online at www.authorsonline.co.uk

ISBN 0 7552 0265 1

Authors OnLine Ltd
19 The Cinques
Gamlingay, Sandy
Bedfordshire SG19 3NU
England

This book is also available in e-book format, details of which are available at www.authorsonline.co.uk

Contents

Introduction

When I was first awakened to my spiritual path I didn't know my aura from my ego, and I had certainly no idea what chakras were. It would have been wonderful to have had a reference book to explain in simple language the meanings of all the new words I was encountering. Well, here it is.

An A to Z of some of the spiritual terminology used by light workers everywhere and all those spiritual people who are quietly working away for the highest good of our Earth. I hope you find it helpful and I send you love and blessings as you raise the light levels of the planet higher each day. May you be like beacons.

Namaste
Sheila

Affirmations

Dictionary ~ *affirmation – the act of affirming or the state of being affirmed. A statement of the truth of something; assertion.*

We are making affirmations all the time whether we realise it or not, and this is what creates our world, our health, our life in general.

It is very important to listen to your self-talk. Just be aware of how you think and speak throughout the day. Is your internal talk positive or negative? You may be surprised to discover that you are directing your life in a very negative way. When listening to yourself, do you hear phrases like - "another horrible day," "I can't do..." whatever, "I never manage to... ," "the world is a terrible place nowadays," "I never have enough money," "I hate... ," "I'm frightened to... ," "nobody cares," "why should I bother, nobody else does," "you don't get anything for nothing," "isn't it awful," "I can't cope" etc. etc.

Try listening to what you are thinking and saying in just one day. You may be surprised to find that you are much more negative than you thought you were. It can be a challenging experience.

Whatever you give your attention to is what you attract in your life.
Do you constantly worry about your weight or

looking fat? You will *continue* to be overweight until you change your mindset and words. When you look in the mirror, what do you see? Do you immediately home in on what you consider to be your 'bad' points? Do you think: "Oh, I hate my nose" or "what a fat lump!" or "you are so ugly" etc. etc. By constantly thinking, saying and therefore *affirming* this, your brain will respond by giving you what you say! Remember, **what you focus on is what you create**.

Try treating yourself with love and respect for a change. Speak lovingly to your reflection. Thank your body every day for being so amazing and so beautiful. It is a miraculous thing after all! Imagine yourself being the shape you'd prefer to be and affirm, "My normal weight is (9 stones or whatever) and that is what I weigh." Or, "Every day I am becoming slimmer and fitter." "I love myself and therefore I treat my body well and feed it only nourishing, healthy foods and beverages."

When you love your body and bless and respect it daily, you will find that you will gradually change any unhealthy eating habits and will reap the benefits by becoming slimmer, fitter and with lots more energy.

Are you constantly fretting about money, or rather, the lack of it? Try affirming daily, "All my needs are met, abundantly." "We live in a rich, abundant universe which has more than enough for all our needs." "Money flows to me, quickly and freely, *and I deserve it*." "I accept my wealth from unexpected sources." "I earn an income of £... per month." *See* the amount of income you choose to receive, in your bank account. *Feel* how you would feel if you had that income. Constantly affirm that you have this money, and it will manifest in your life.

Of course, if you follow that affirmation by silently thinking, "But that won't happen to me," or "this won't work – it never does," then it won't! You are suffering from self sabotage and you need to address the underlying issues before you can move forward. If you feel unable to resolve things for yourself after realising what you are doing, then perhaps a visit to a therapist would be helpful. I recommend Emotional Freedom Technique (EFT), Sekhem or Hypnotherapy.

Here are some affirmations which you might like to repeat often:-

I am healthy and have abundant energy.
I have harmonious relationships.
All my needs are met.
I love and approve of myself. All is well in my world.
I am fulfilling my life purpose and feel great joy.

Angels

Dictionary ~ angel – *one of a class of spiritual beings attendant upon God. In medieval angelology they are divided by rank into nine orders. A divine messenger from God. A guardian spirit. A conventional representation of any of these beings, depicted in human form with wings.*

And the angel came in unto her, and said, ' Hail, thou that art highly favoured, the Lord is with thee: blessed art thou among women.' And when she saw him, she was troubled at his saying, and cast in her mind what manner of salutation this should be. And the angel said unto her, 'Fear not, Mary, for thou hast found favour with God. And behold, thou shalt conceive in thy womb and bring forth a son, and you shall call his name Jesus.'
Luke, 1:28 – 31

Up until a few years ago, I hadn't ever thought of angels as beings which are around us in this day and age. I thought they were something which you could read about in the bible stories but were probably just a myth. How wrong I was!

One day, I was sitting reading an article in a magazine, which was talking about guardian angels and explained that it was easy to contact them and if you wanted to know the name of your angel, just to ask. Well, I didn't do anything special – no meditation or sacred words – I just sat there and said, ' OK Guardian Angel, what is your name please' or something like that, and immediately I 'felt' a name at my right ear and thought it was Michael. I repeated, 'Is it Michael?' and straight away got the name MICAH printed in red block capitals in front of my eyes! I felt elated and astounded that I'd actually received a communication. Of course, later on, I managed to convince myself that I'd just imagined it.

My interest in angels had been awakened however, and I booked to go on an angel workshop and read lots of literature on the subject of angels. It seemed that hundreds of people all over the world were having experiences of angel visits and messages. At the workshop, we were led in meditation to meet our guardian or companion angels, and when it was time to ask their name, I got – 'Micah, Micah, it's me Micah' over and over again! I could feel him standing on my left. I've never been privileged to see his face (yet) but I *know* he is there.

Angels are pure spirit so don't have a form, but they appear to us in a way that we can recognise. People who have seen them report that they are usually shining beings of humanoid appearance. They are often hovering just above the ground and some have wings and others don't. They are androgynous but generally have the appearance of a male or a female. They work in a very gentle way and would never do anything to frighten or alarm us. They gently impress our thoughts with suggestions to help us, and of course, we think that we thought up everything by ourselves! We are constantly being divinely inspired.

Angels are a separate evolution from humans, so humans don't become angels when they die, for example, as some people imagine; however, I know from experiences and discussions that many angels have opted to incarnate as humans in this time, so it seems to work the opposite way. Angels are coming down into the density of our planet to become humans. One of my close friends is one such person; she is a teacher at the moment in a secondary school. One day a pupil left a drawing she'd done of an angel on my friend's desk saying, "That's you, miss" as she walked away. The young girl had obviously been able to see the angelic quality shining through my friend.

Our guardian or companion angels are allotted to us from birth. Most people have just one guardian angel, while others have two. Sometimes they appear as a male and a female energy. They will never ever interfere in our lives but will assist us if invited. The only time they will come in unasked is if we are about to do something which would end our life before our appointed time. There are many stories of people having amazing escapes from death and feeling physically lifted by invisible hands.

If you are having difficulties or a conflict with someone, or perhaps communication has broken down, ask your guardian angel to speak with the other person's angel about the situation and to help resolve things for the highest good of all concerned. You will find that there will be a change of heart and you will both be able to settle matters amicably.

Here is an extract from a message channelled from the angels through Laura Newbury.

"Direct light around yourself as much as possible and tell your friends to do this also – by friends we mean those whom you know to be on this path and those who are awake and aware... If you surround yourself with light, then you are protected; we can reach you far more easily and impart the necessary information to each one of you, for it is at this time that Heaven awaits for those who are able and willing to seek the truth. They shall be given the ability to manifest their gifts in this world, and their abilities will become tenfold, if they work with the light. For all negativity will fall away, and that energy which bound itself and the person concerned to darkness will emerge as positive and work towards the healing of the world. Faith is necessary, and we stress that time is short; it will require a leap of faith for many to do this.

We believe it possible though. We remind you that the transformation always takes place from the heart, and there may be no outward sign of change except that the person concerned will feel differently. Forgiveness is a necessary step, and patience (which is your new challenge) and overall there is a need for trust.

These are all difficult areas for those who have dwelt in fear, but it is necessary to understand that fear is illusion, and can be cast out and when that happens, Love will abound.

Love is the key and many hold the key, not knowing that it is connected with a door; that is the door we call "forgiveness." It is only possible to find the door if the key is held by those of a pure heart, those who are able to love unconditionally all things of the world. Love will draw them to the door and trust is the drive which will push them through. Once through, then they are

in the Light and have come home. Then they can truly work for the Light and Glory of God."

Apparently, the angels use tiny white feathers as their calling cards! I felt very sceptical of this as I live in a coastal village and there are many white seagull feathers around. However, I asked to be given an angel feather and knew that it would have to be found somewhere that there would be no chance of finding a feather normally – like when making the bed for example. I saw many white feathers, but disregarded them until one day, I threw open a lace tablecloth over my dining table, and there, from the centre, rose a perfect little white feather. It hadn't been there when I ironed the cloth earlier. Emotion rose within me and I smiled and just *knew* this was my confirmation. From that day, I've kept beautiful white feathers which I've been privileged to be given by the angels, in a special box which I've covered with angel pictures.

Try it out for yourself. Just ask the angels to give you proof and to send you a white feather. You'll know when you find one in some unusual place that you have your confirmation. Many of my friends have had feathers which they feel gave them comfort or perhaps an acknowledgement of work well done, or made them feel uplifted.

One morning, my husband called upstairs to me, that Muffin, our little black cat, was missing. I knew that something bad must have happened to her as she never left our garden. It has a high wall around it and we thought she was too fat and lazy to climb over. However, something must have enticed her to jump over the wall. I dressed quickly, ran out of the front door and turned to the right, while my husband went to the left to search for her. My eyes were immediately drawn to a trail of white feathers on the ground. We have a church hall next door and the feathers were leading me up the side of the building like the pebbles in 'Babes in the Wood'. I hurried on, following the feathers and came to a small raised flower bed. It looked empty, but when I called, 'Muffin!' a little black head was lifted up and a pitiful mewing ensued. I found our little cat, badly injured... she must have been hit by a car and couldn't make it back over the wall. We got her to the vet's where she was treated, but sadly died a few days later from internal bleeding. I still vividly recall the trail of white feathers which led me to her quickly though, and know that the angels were helping me that morning.

I know two ladies who are now my friends, who were coming to me for a consultation because one of them had been having messages from an angel, and she had written down pages and pages of communications from the angel. She was very sceptical and doubted what was happening to her. Somehow, she was lead to speak to me about her channelled writing and I managed to convince her that what she was experiencing was real. On the journey to my home, suddenly, thousands of white feathers had been 'thrown' at the car windscreen – just like a snowstorm! My friends expected to see a lorry loaded with turkeys or something just ahead, but there was only normal traffic. They concluded that it was a sign from the angels that they were doing the right thing in coming to see me! I was astounded myself when I heard this story. What on earth could I do? I wasn't an authority on angels. We decided just to 'go with the flow' and we sat and talked and I led them in a guided visualisation to meet their guardian angels. Then I offered myself as a channel and gave both the ladies messages which turned out to be very pertinent. Then I received a message for myself which resulted in this book being written! The angel I channelled was Archangel Raphael.

There are many books now available about angels as more and more people are becoming aware of them in their lives. If you need help of any kind from finding a lost object to selling your house, to help with an emotional problem then just ask the angels to guide you. It should be done in a polite, respectful way and remember to give thanks. The angels will always come to your assistance when asked. There are plumber angels and computer angels as well as angels for children and animals etc.

Every blade of grass has its Angel that bends over it and whispers, 'Grow, grow.'
The Talmud

Each time you hear an ambulance or fire engine passing, just direct the angels of love and light to go and help in any way they can for the highest good. Whenever there is bad news on the television, send angels to the situation. This is the planet of choice and the angels cannot intervene unless we ask them to. Most people don't realise this. There are millions of angels just waiting to be directed by us. They will never intervene without permission.

[In Heaven are] the archangels who are above angels...and the angels who are appointed over seasons and years, the angels who are over rivers and sea, and who are over the fruits of the earth, and the angels who are over every grass, giving food to all, to every living thing, and the angels who

write all the souls of men...; in their midst are six Phoenixes and six Cherubim and six six-winged ones continually with one voice singing...
The Book of the Secrets of Enoch, X1X:3

It is generally accepted that there is a hierarchy in the angelic realms.

Our **guardian** angels or companion angels as they have come to be known, reside in the First Sphere which is nearest to us, along with the **Archangels** who oversee large groups of angels, and the names you will be most familiar with are Michael, Gabriel, Raphael and Uriel. However there are hundreds of Archangels. Beyond the Archangels are the **Principalities** who are the guardians of larger groups of humanity such as multi national corporations and cities.

Next comes the Second Sphere. There are angels called **Powers,** who hold the collective history of all humanity. Then the **Virtues,** who send us divine energy. Then the **Dominions**, who are heavenly governors working to integrate the spiritual and earthly worlds.

In the Third Sphere, dwell the **Thrones** or planetary angels. There is an Earth angel who oversees our planet. It is very helpful in these times to communicate with Earth angel and ask the angelic realms to help lessen the effects of earthquakes and tidal waves etc. Higher still are the **Cherubim,** the guardians of the stars. They send us divine light. Nearest to God are the **Seraphim** who regulate the movement of the heavens and sing the music of the spheres.

Are there really all these echelons or has mankind given the angelic beings job descriptions? I don't know, but I do know that when we communicate with angels, we receive an answer.

There are two angels, that attend unseen
Each one of us, and in the great books record
Our good and evil deeds. He who writes down
The good ones, after every action closes
His volume, and ascends with it to God.
The other keeps his dreadful day-book open
Till sunset, that we may repent; which doing
The record of the action fades away,
And leaves a line of white across the page.
Henry Wadsworth Longfellow, Christus

Try writing to your companion angel. Gather your notepad and pen and settle yourself quietly. You may like to light a candle (I always do this whenever I'm working in my therapy room or meditating. To me, it symbolises that I am working in the Light) and/or burn incense.

Write a letter to your angel starting, Dear... and ending in the way that you would write to a dear friend. You will probably want to ask a question. Once you have written your letter, sit quietly and prepare a new page. Start writing a letter to yourself. You will feel inspired to write. The pen won't start writing by itself! *You* will have to write and at first, you will think that you have just made it all up. However, you will probably find that the style of speech or the grammar is different from your own. Sign off. What has your angel said? I was convinced it was just me who had written the letter the first time I did this, until I read the ending. It was signed off: 'Walk in the Light'. I would never have written that.

Here is a fun angel visualisation which you may like to try with a group of friends. One person will need to direct the proceedings. You need to stand in a tight circle all facing in the same direction, looking at the back of the person in front of you. Now gently rub and smooth with your hands over the shoulder blade area, starting to imagine wings. The person behind you will be rubbing *your* shoulder blades. Try to get an impression of wings. What size are they? Do they just come to the waist, or do they go all the way to the ground? How widespread are they? What colour are they? Close your eyes and 'see' with your inner eyes and begin to gently brush the wings and feel the texture. Now you are ready to fly with the angels. Invite your companion angel to hold your left hand, and ask another angel to come in and hold your right hand. Now, you are going to fly with the angels, so imagine flexing your wings for a few moments, then take a small jump off the floor, then another jump... and now you are flying up through the ceiling and out into the air, held securely by the two angels. It can be daytime or night, whichever you choose. Feel the air rushing past your face and look down over familiar surroundings. Now gradually let go of the angel who is holding you on the right, then let go of your guardian angel's hand. You are flying by yourself! You can go anywhere in the world that you desire. Choose somewhere on earth that needs love and help and you can instantly fly there. You have a basket of rose petals with you. Sprinkle some of the petals over the area which needs your help. Do you have a friend or relative who is ill or distressed? Fly to where they are and sprinkle some rose petals over their abode. Now go to your own home and shower the remaining petals over your own home and garden, then gradually fly back to where you started from and bring yourself back to full awareness in the room. Stamp your feet firmly on the floor to make sure you are grounded, and then have a discussion with your friends. Have fun finding out where you've all flown to and comparing thoughts on the size and colours of your wings.

Angels can fly because they take themselves lightly.
G.K. Chesterton, Orthodoxy

One of the most memorable times I have regarding angels was when I had the privilege to attend a week long conference called 'Angels 2000' at the Findhorn Community, in the north of Scotland. My friend and I stayed in a turf roofed chalet which we shared with people from as far off as Australia. There were in the region of 300 folk attending the conference from all over the world. British people were definitely in the minority .There were many who couldn't speak any English and had to use interpreters for the entire week. I found it incredible that so many people were prepared to travel half way round the globe for a conference on Angels!

It was Easter weekend and the weather was glorious. There were spectacular spring flower arrangements abounding and everyone was very friendly. There were speakers and renowned authors holding workshops: Diana Cooper, Caroline Myss, William Bloom and Sandra Ingerman, to name but a few.

After a wonderful opening ceremony on Easter Sunday, I made my way to the sand dunes where a huge bonfire was lit and some of the participants joined in circle dancing. Thanks and praise was given to the salamanders (spirits of the fire) and the whole spectacle was amazing. While all this was going on, some ladies dressed as angels in white costumes with wings, circulated throughout the crowds with large baskets of beautifully decorated hard boiled eggs, and apples for those who preferred them. I chose a lovely brown egg with a gold design like a cross painted on it. It was so beautiful I couldn't bear to break it and eat it, so I kept it and I still have it. The 'angels' quietly moved among the people for the rest of the week, bringing a cushion here and a drink of water there; a lovely way to show us how our own angels support us unobtrusively.

Workshops and talks were held each morning, afternoon and evening as each speaker told their own angel stories and gave us their own interpretation of the angelic realms. To some, the nature spirits and fairies are considered to be angels. The shamans and the Native American peoples have yet another view. We had a wonderful week of experiential workshops and music and dance.

One evening, we had a fancy-dress masked ball, where everyone had to dress as angels, fairies or nature spirits. The costumes were fantastic and so imaginative. I dressed as a sea nymph, with a floaty blue dress covered in netting with shells and seaweed attached. There were lots of flower fairies, angels with lovely wings and the men favoured Pan and Green Man. The fun part for me was that we were required to wear masks! It gave the feeling of being invisible! I could walk around and no one recognised me. A wonderful week which I will remember forever.

Angels are showering us with blessings all the time. Make time to communicate and thank them. You will soon find so many little 'coincidences' and synchronicities happening as you go with the flow and follow your intuition. I believe that we have all been positioned where we need to be now. Life will continue to have good days and not so good days, but with the comfort, support and help of the angels, we can all help to raise the vibration of our planet.

Here are the words to a song which I brought through from the angels:

Michael, Gabriel, Raphael and Uriel
Surround me and astound me with your loving
wings
Guide me, protect me, heal me and teach me
To reflect, in my life, only beautiful things.

Ascended Masters

The Ascended Masters are highly evolved beings, also known as the Illumined Ones, who have gone before us. They can communicate telepathically with those people whose vibrations are high enough to receive their messages.

According to Diana Cooper in, 'A Little Light on Ascension', "As more individuals are becoming enlightened and dedicating themselves to the spiritual path, the Illumined Ones are able to impress or channel through them great waves of light, hope, inspiration and truth. When we are ready for the responsibility which is inherent in working with the Illumined Ones they will guide and assist us in our evolution. In the past this is something that only happened to the very few who were aware and pure enough to tune in to their broadcast. Now it is available to us as soon as we raise our vibrational frequency high enough.

There are thousands of Ascended Masters from different cultures and various parts of the universes and some are working specifically for our planet."

Let me mention a few now. The following information is extracted from 'A New Light on Ascension' by Diana Cooper. "**El Morya** is known as the Chohan of the First Ray. He works closely with Archangel Michael. As Abraham, he shaped the early Semite races and has subsequently influenced their evolution. He will help them to integrate with other races as their learning and work is complete on Earth.

At the fall of Atlantis, he carried its knowledge and wisdom to the Euphrates and was instrumental in establishing the Mesopotamian civilisation. He oversaw the development of their script so that they could keep records on clay tablets. He has also helped to develop the Islamic faith and its art.

It was El Morya who first recognised the cosmic power of transmutation held by water and he introduced the concept of baptism. With Lord Kuthumi, he influenced Madam Blavatsky's writings and prompted her to develop the Theosophical Society.

El Morya is working very closely with Earth to help us during this time of massive change. He is a member of the Great White Brotherhood and originates from Mercury. He will shortly undertake a major role, becoming the *Manu*, which means 'perfect man'. It is on the qualities and characteristics of the Manu that the new root race of humanity, 'the sixth root race' will be based.

His past incarnations include Melchior, one of the three wise men, Abraham, the founder of the Jewish religion, Akbar the Great, King Solomon and King Arthur.

Lord Kuthumi still shares the role of World Teacher in the inner planes with Sananda, though he will soon take on full responsibility for this mighty task. As Head of the Schools of Learning, he is very interested in all who are teaching the spiritual truths. One of his tasks is to transform dogmatic thinking in religion so that unconditional love can manifest. There are 12,000 beings working with him, in spirit or in body, to bring this about.

His lives have demonstrated love to all. He was a

founder member of the Knights Templar, who kept ancient esoteric secrets and protected pilgrims. As Pythagoras he introduced sacred geometry, numerology, mathematics and the music of the spheres to the world and also formed a mystery school for the Great White Brotherhood. As St. Francis of Assisi, he demonstrated harmlessness and love to all creatures. As Shah Jahan, he built the Taj Mahal as an offering of perfect love to his wife. He was John the Beloved; Balthazar, the Wise Man who divined the birthplace of Jesus; and Tutmoses 111 of Egypt. This mighty being is the Doorkeeper of the ancient occult mysteries and is now bringing forward esoteric information to receptive lightworkers as our planet moves forward on its Ascension pathway.

Serapis Bey is now an initiate of the Third Ray and has moved to the position of Chohan of the Fourth Ray – the ray of harmony and balance. He originated from Venus and is the only Master to work with the Seraphim on their devic and angelic evolution. He works on the amethyst and violet rays, the rays of the Age of Aquarius.

He has an ascension chamber in Luxor and is know as The Egyptian because he worked with the angels to influence the building of the Pyramids, where his teachings are said to be hidden. His new role is to establish higher healing in medicine, including using sound waves and lasers. He will also encourage Aquarian Age thinking and learning. In previous incarnations he was a great priest Avatar in Atlantis and Keeper of the White Flame. He was also Zoroaster. In Egyptian incarnations he was Akhenaton 1V, the Pharaoh who protected and reorganised the Great White Brotherhood and also established new rules for it. At that time he tried to end the role of the corrupt priesthood and bring back an understanding of the one God. He was also the Pharaoh Amenophis, who built the temple of Thebes.

Hilarion remains for the time being as Chohan of the Fifth ray, which is orange. He also works with yellow to stimulate an understanding of practical and esoteric science for the New Age. He directs his energy to help those who wish to become higher channels and clairvoyants. His previous incarnations were in Atlantis, where he worked in the Temple of Truth and in Greece where he established the Oracle of Delphi. He was Paul, the Apostle. He works closely with Master Marko who represents the highest Galactic confederation of our solar system - the capital of the Solar systems on Saturn. He is also the negotiator on Earth on the Council of Saturn so that we remain connected to our Spiritual journey.

Jesus /Sananda who was the Chohan or Master of the Sixth Ray, is still co-sharing the position of World Teacher with Lord Kuthumi during a hand-over period. He is also working beside Lord Maitreya as Overlord for the planet. He is known as Sananda in the inner planes and is the most well known and beloved of all the Illumined Ones.

He is one of twelve sons/daughters of God and the only one to incarnate on our planet. In his lifetime as Jesus he was an Essene and became a high priest in the Order of Melchizedek. He was specifically prepared before birth and during his lifetime to become the Christ of the Age. When he was ready to take in the energy of the Cosmic Christ, Lord Maitreya worked through him. He originated from Venus with no karma to resolve. His previous incarnations include Adam, Enoch, Jeshua, Joshua,

Elijah and Joseph of Egypt. He also reincarnated as Apollonius of Tyana, a great Master continuing to teach Divine Laws. His life as Jesus was the only one in which the entire soul energy came to Earth.

St. Germain was the Chohan of the Seventh Ray, the violet ray, who brought to us the Violet Flame of purification. The aspect of him that incarnated as Rakoczy has recently taken over Master of the Eleventh Ray. St. Germain's previous incarnations include Samuel the prophet, Lao-Tze, the Chinese philosopher; Joseph of Nazareth, St. Alban; Proclus, the Greek philosopher; Merlin the Magician, Christopher Columbus, Francis Bacon, Rakoczy. As Christian Rosenkreutz, he founded the Order of the Rosy Cross, which later became the Rosicrucians."

Mother Mary is more commonly known as the Virgin Mary. "In Lemuria she incarnated as *Mar-ra*, meaning 'the goddess who is the mother of the sun'. She was the first initiate of that civilisation and developed the Lemurian Mystery School. Later she was the first Lemurian to ascend from Earth.

In Atlantis she was Isis, the High Priestess of Atlantis, who gave virgin birth to Horus, the Sun God, who represents the solar logos. (In Egypt Horus was known as the Lion King.) At the start of the Piscean age, born of Essene parents, she was prepared as a pure vestal virgin for the virgin birth of Jesus, who was the Christ of his time. Now she is working with the team of Illumined Ones to re-empower women and bring back the Divine Feminine wisdom to Earth."

Kwan Yin, Guanyin or Quan Yin is the eastern equivalent of Mother Mary helping to bring in Goddess energy to the planet. Originally, Kwan Yin was a male Indian deity known as Avalokitesvara and when Buddhism came from India to Tibet and then moved into China gradually, over time, the Chinese mingled the new religion with their own beliefs and customs and Avalokitesvara's male image changed into the present day Goddess of Mercy and Mother of Compassion, Kwan Yin. She is usually depicted wearing white and is associated with a five petalled lotus.

I feel particularly connected to Kwan Yin and to Jesus. I was brought up knowing and loving Jesus from childhood. I felt the connection with Kwan Yin when I learned a form of healing called Magnified Healing. I have a picture of Kwan Yin in my therapy room and her statue stands under a willow tree in my garden and I have a beautiful white porcelain statuette which a friend bought for me in Shanghai, in my dining room, so she is never far from my thoughts.

Astral Travel

Have you ever found yourself deep in thought, imagining you are someplace other than where you are; perhaps your home town, your parents' house, a favourite holiday destination? Everything seems so real, and you can hear the sounds and smell the smells? That is a form of astral travel.

Some people are very skilled at it, and can 'visit' another place, perhaps to check that everything is safe, or to see a loved one who is ill for example. It can happen that you think of someone and they later tell you that they had been thinking about being in your home, visiting you. They can tell you what your furnishings look like, or describe your kitchen or whatever, even though they have never been in your home before. They have astral travelled to you and you have picked that up when they popped into your mind.

We all astral travel each night when we go to sleep. We leave our physical bodies behind with just enough energy to maintain them, while we return to Source to be re-energised. Some of us have work which we do out in the cosmos, and other times we may be visiting with loved ones who have made their transition. We have no memory of this when we return to our bodies, but sometimes we may have fleeting glimpses of what we have been doing, but presume it is all a dream which disappears quickly once we awaken.

24

The most common recorded form of astral travel is an 'out of body experience' most usually, a Near Death Experience. This most often happens when someone is on the operating table in hospital, or just after an accident when they experience their consciousness coming out of their body and floating above the scene. When they return to their body, they can recall all the events that were happening round about them and relay them accurately, even though they were unconscious or apparently, dead. There are many books and articles written about this type of experience.

Atlantis

Dictionary: *(in ancient legend) a continent said to have sunk beneath the Atlantic west of Gibraltar.*

The location of Atlantis has never been found. The first reference to this lost continent was by Plato the Greek philosopher around 360BC who wrote about Atlantis in his work, *Timaeus and Critias,* describing that it had disappeared beneath the waves due to an earthquake around 9000BC.

Many people liken this to the story of Noah and the Flood in the Old Testament. Some remnants of the land of Atlantis are said to be in the Azores, the Canaries and the Bahamas.

There are people today who believe they have memories of their past lives, and can remember a life or lifetimes in Atlantis. As the civilisation is thought to have lasted for 250,000 years, it is probable that all the people who are incarnated at this present time have had lifetimes in Atlantis.

It was said to be a very highly evolved civilisation, far more advanced than we are now. The lifestyle was simple and the people lived closely with nature, enjoying a peaceful, happy existence. Colour, crystals and sound were used for maintaining good health. Technology was very advanced and telekinesis and sound were used to transport stones used in building.

Although complete proof of the existence of Atlantis has yet to be found, there are now many books available on the subject, and much research being done to try to prove once and for all that Atlantis is not just a myth.

Aura

Dictionary ~ aura – *any invisible emanation, especially surrounding a person or object.*

The aura is the energy field surrounding all living things. Some people are able to see the aura with the naked eye but most people have to develop this skill. The energy field surrounding a human body will normally be in an egg shape approximately 4 feet around the body, but can extend to 30 feet or more. Remember this is above, below, in front and behind. The aura contains colours which are moving and changing all the time, depending on our thoughts and feelings in any given moment. You can have your aura photographed by Kirlian photography, but remember that the picture shows the way your energy field is at that moment only. Some people will say, 'I have a blue aura' or 'I have a pink aura' but this is not strictly true as the colours will change frequently as I mentioned before.

It is possible to train yourself to see the energy fields around people, plants, animals etc.

To see the aura of another person, first of all have them standing or seated in front of a plain wall, with lighting which does not cast a shadow on the wall behind them. Focus your vision on their forehead or solar plexus area for a few moments and then allow your eyes to go out of focus. Keeping your eyes 'soft', be aware of their whole body with your peripheral vision. At first, your eyes may water, and you may find it hard to relax and let your eyes encompass the whole body, but gradually, you may start to pick up areas of soft colour. The temptation is to immediately focus on the colour, and then of course it disappears. You will soon learn to control the urge to look at the colour and just take it all in passively. You will also begin to see the etheric layer which may appear as a white or silvery layer like a silhouette surrounding the whole body. With practice, you will become much more aware of auras and will begin to see them around trees and flowers as well as people.

The aura is composed of seven different layers, not like an onion, but continually penetrating and interpenetrating the physical body and this is explained in great depth by Barbara Ann Brennan in her book, 'Light Emerging - The Journey of Personal Healing'. I will keep things simple however, and my understanding is that the first level of the energy field is called the etheric body, and then comes the emotional body, then the mental body, then the astral body, then three spiritual bodies.

We are really massive, amazing beings who have chosen this physical form for this lifetime and this small dense physical body is encompassed in the beautiful, weaving light of our energy bodies.

As we meet and interact with other humans, we take in energy and information from them and they do likewise with us. When we are well and strong, our auras are vibrant and clear. When we fall ill, there may be holes or dark areas which are apparent in our auras. An energy healing treatment such as Sekhem, Reiki or Spiritual Healing, will heal those tears or holes.

Have you ever been standing somewhere and had the feeling that someone was watching you and when you turned round, there was? Our aura can act like antennae and we can sense when someone is in our energy field. You might like to try out the following techniques to measure the aura.

You can dowse with rods (see the chapter on Dowsing) to find out where someone's aura starts.

You might also like to try this. Have someone stand with their back to you. Now move quite close to them and perform a pushing action with your hands towards their back. Don't actually touch them, and don't say what you are doing, just push the air with intention. After a few moments, they will generally start to sway or fall forwards. You could then try 'pulling' them backwards and see what happens. Have fun with it!

Ayurveda

Pronounced *eye-yer-veh-dah,* Ayurveda is from the ancient Indian language Sanskrit and literally means 'knowledge of life'. It is an all-embracing system of medicine which deals with every aspect of health: physical, mental and spiritual.

It all begins with knowing yourself. The Ayurvedic approach involves addressing the unique needs of your individual body. Recognising and balancing your mental and emotional states while deepening your connection with your spiritual self. This is a personal journey as you are the only one who will suffer from your neglect or benefit from your attentions.

According to Ayurvedic teaching, everything in the universe consists of three basic elements or forces. In Sanskrit, they are called, <u>Vata</u>, <u>Pitta</u> and <u>Kapha</u>. Vata is likened to the wind, being constantly on the move, and controls the central nervous system. Pitta is a source of energy like the sun, and controls the digestion and all biochemical processes. Kapha governs the balance of tissue fluid, controlling cell growth and is likened to the moon.

Good health results when the three forces are in harmony. When you become aware of these three qualities in yourself, you take the first steps towards creating a healthy life. Ayurveda shows you how to identify these forces in your own unique body, and to work with them and gain freedom from their limitations.

The Ayurvedic practitioner will endeavour to discover the client's own inherent disposition and pinpoint any area of physical or mental imbalance.

<u>Vata</u> imbalance can be caused by eating irregularly, not having enough sleep, a promiscuous sex life, bad temper outbursts and overworking or overexertion of any kind.

<u>Pitta</u> imbalance can be caused by indigestion, acidity, feelings of grief or fear and alcohol abuse.

<u>Kapha</u> imbalance can be caused by insufficient physical exercise, sleeping during the day and sometimes the changing effects of the seasons.

Taking into account the person's age and lifestyle, the practitioner will help to bring balance back into their life by counteracting the destructive forces with positive action, thereby creating vibrant health.

Blessing

Dictionary ~ noun: *the act of invoking divine protection or aid ~ the words or ceremony used for this ~ a short prayer used before or after a meal; grace ~ approval, good wishes ~ the bestowal of a divine gift or favour ~ a happy event.* verb ~ *to give honour or glory to (a person or thing) as holy ~ to call upon God to protect ~ to grant happiness, health or prosperity to.*

You may have often heard the phrase, "Count your blessings" but how many of you have actually done that!

It is an excellent practice to think of, and, even better, write down at least five blessings that you have in your life at the end of each day. There is so much for which to be thankful. It helps to bring you back into the 'now' and keeps your thoughts away from all the negativity we are fed through the media.

Bless your food. You can do it mentally if it is not appropriate to speak out loud. Give thanks for the food and ask that it nourish every cell, molecule and electron of your body.

Bless your water. We are so fortunate in the UK to still have water readily available for our use. I recommend that you read the books by Masaru Emoto about the way water can change depending upon the intention that goes into it. As our bodies are over 60% water, we are greatly affected by the thoughts, words and vibes constantly bombarding us throughout each day. Put a label on your water jug and kettle, with words like, Blessings, Love and Gratitude, Thanks. The quality of the water will be greatly enhanced.

Bless your body. Work through each part of yourself from your toes to your hair! Give thanks to the foot or whatever, for being so miraculous and working so hard for you. Bless each tiny area of your body. I guarantee that by the time you have finished, you will feel marvellous!

Bless your house, bless your work, bless your car - bless everything in your life!

Sometimes, when life is proving to be very challenging, it can be hard to see the blessings in a situation.

Sir Winston Churchill once said, "If this is a blessing, it is certainly very well disguised." However, as you look in hindsight, you will find that even the most agonising situation had a blessing disguised within it.

Try to *give* a blessing to someone in your life each day, or *be* a blessing to them. A little act of kindness can mean such a lot. We are receiving divine blessings all the time, and sometimes don't even notice ...the perfect flower just opened, the sight of a baby bird learning to fly, the glimpse of a wild animal, a stunning sunset, the laughter of a child, the smile from a friend, the kind touch of a loved one, the list could go on and on...**YOU ARE BLESSED**.

Boundaries

Dictionary: *something that indicates the farthest limit, as of an area; border.*

I'm sure you can all relate to the feeling of someone 'invading your space.' We each have an area around us where, if someone crosses that line, we feel threatened and vulnerable. We need to be positive and strong and state clearly exactly what we are prepared to accept from another person.

Do you find it hard to say 'No' then feel 'put upon' and 'hard done by?' You will continue to act like a doormat and become thoroughly worn down unless you make your boundaries clear. It may help to write down what you are prepared to accept. Draw a circle on a piece of paper and within the circle write down the things you wish to allow through: love, work, friendship and so on. Just outside the circle, write down the things which you will accept by invitation: new acquaintances, job opportunities, requests for help, criticism etc. The circle acts like a shield which reflects your desires and wishes for your life at an unconscious level. Outside the boundary you are making clear what you wish to experience on your terms.

If someone asks you to do something which you definitely don't want to do, in future, just say, "No, I can't do that for you" or something similar. Say it with a smile, and there is no need to justify yourself by giving reasons why you can't do it! People are generally quite happy to know exactly where they stand and so long as you are polite, no offence will be taken.

Be like the Armadillo of Native American teachings and wear your armour on your back. Any harsh words or negativity will just roll off. **Set your boundaries and you will not feel invaded.**

Breath

Dictionary: *a single respiration or inhalation of air ~ life, energy or vitality.*

It is interesting to find that the Hebrew word for spirit is *ruach,* which means "air in motion". It is also the same word for "breath" and also for "life". Our English word "spirit" does not give the full emphasis of these different meanings.

In Genesis 2:6-7 we read, " And the Lord God formed man of the dust of the ground and breathed into his nostrils the breath of life; and man became a living being" (or living soul).

We were created from the breath of God according to the Bible.

The Greek word pneuma means a current of air, breath, a breeze or spirit. Both the Hebrew and Greek words create a more comprehensive meaning of what breath is.

The whole of mankind and the animal kingdom need to breathe air in order to stay alive. It is the first thing a baby does when born – takes its first gasp of air and then continues breathing for a lifetime until one day, the breath stops. We tend to take this part of our system completely for granted as we go about our daily tasks and our lungs continue to breathe automatically without our having to tell them!

Some babies have a traumatic birth and this can sometimes cause them to gasp in air at birth and try to hold it. This pattern of holding the breath continues into adulthood and usually goes unnoticed. A trained therapist can help to correct this situation and retrain the body to breathe in the correct way. Asthmatics will find that some help from a Buteyko therapist may alleviate their breathing difficulties.

'Watching the breath' is a very simple way of relaxing and allowing yourself to go into a meditative state. Just sit comfortably with your back straight, still your body, and focus your thoughts on your breath. Just watch it going in through your nose and into your lungs, then out again. Don't try to change anything, just observe. You will find that you can calm your thoughts and feel relaxed yet energised.

Psalm 150 *"Let everything that has breath praise the Lord. Praise the Lord!"*

Chakras

Chakra means; *a spinning wheel or vortex* in Sanskrit.

The chakras are energy centres in the etheric, invisible to the naked eye, which run in line with our spines. They are conical like a funnel and spin, drawing in energy or *prana*, and distributing it to the associated glands and organs in our physical bodies. If a chakra stops functioning properly due to physical or emotional trauma, the corresponding part of the body will weaken and illness can follow.

The positions of the seven main chakras are as follows:

The **Base** chakra is positioned at the perineum, or more usually just called the coccyx area. There is only one chakra here, corresponding to the crown chakra at the other end of the spinal cord.

It vibrates with the colour **Red** and is associated with the lower parts of the body, the genitals and the kidneys. It governs the adrenal glands and is connected to our basic survival needs and physical vitality.

The **Sacral** chakra is just below the navel at the front and straight through at the back. It vibrates with the colour **Orange** and is associated with the pelvic area, the reproductive system and all organs in that area. It governs the ovaries and testes and is concerned with our sexuality and sensuality.

The **Solar Plexus** chakra is placed in the centre just below the ribcage at the front, and at the corresponding point on the back, just below the shoulder blades. It vibrates with the colour **Yellow** and supplies energy to our stomach, liver, gall bladder, pancreas, spleen and is where we hold our self esteem and centre of power. It governs the pancreas.

The **Heart** chakra is found in the middle of the chest, in the centre of the breastbone at the front and in the middle of the shoulder blades at the back. It vibrates to the colour **Green** and is the centre where we feel love, compassion and will. The front aspect is of love and the back aspect is will. This chakra governs the thymus gland and feeds energy to the heart, lungs and circulatory system.

The **Throat** chakra is positioned at the front of the throat in the region of the adam's apple and at the back of the neck. It vibrates with **Blue** and is the centre for self expression, creativity and speaking the truth. It relates to the senses of smelling, tasting and hearing and feeds energy to the throat, mouth and respiratory system. It governs the thyroid gland.

The **Third Eye** chakra is in the centre of the forehead at the front and at the occipital bump at the back of the head. It vibrates with the colour **Indigo** and governs the Pituitary gland. It supplies energy to the lower brain, the ears, nose, the left eye and the nervous system. It is associated with sight and clairvoyance, intuition and intellect.

The **Crown** chakra is positioned at the centre of the top of the head. One only. It vibrates with the colour **Violet** or some say, **White.** It is related to the upper brain and the right eye. It governs the Pineal gland, and is where we integrate personality with spirituality. We connect with our Higher Self.

There are other minor chakras throughout the body, such as at the knees and hands, but those mentioned above are the main energy centres.

Channelling

Dictionary: *a means or agency of access, communication.*

The form of channelling with which most people are familiar is energy healing such as Reiki, Seichim, Sekhem and Spiritual Healing. The *channel* or practitioner/therapist simply acts as a conduit for the healing energy which is passed on to the recipient through the hands. The practitioner is not doing the healing; the person receiving the Divine energy is the one who is doing the healing! The practitioner is simply 'a piece of plumber's pipe' receiving and passing on the healing energy.

Many people channel through their voices and pass on messages from Spirit Guides, Ascended Masters, Angels, Star Beings or other entities from different planes of existence. If you are the recipient of a channelled message, use your discernment and 'feel' for yourself if it is the truth. There are a lot of people out there working from ego, but there are just as many genuine lightworkers who are bringing through vital messages of encouragement and wisdom. There are many valuable channelled books on the market worth reading. Of course, the internet is full of channelled messages. On reading any of them, if you find that you get lost or bored half way through the page and only a small proportion of the piece rings true with you, then disregard it. Take on board only that which resonates with you. Don't be taken in by anything which instils fear, for example.

It is thought that Gene Roddenberry, the creator of Star Trek, channelled or was divinely inspired with the information for the series. The plan being that, as interstellar travel and 'aliens' became the norm on television- which it has with many films and programmes about star beings - we would not be surprised when they really manifest. Many people feel that they are being inspired by great musicians like Mozart or artists like Rembrandt. Perhaps they are.

If you find that you start to receive guidance or messages by clairaudience or you are inspired to write down information, it is advisable to check the source of your channelling. Ask who is speaking through you. Ask if they are working totally for the Light. Challenge them three times and by spiritual law, they must answer truthfully. If they are not working for the Light, they will leave. All angels, ascended masters or any beings of Light will be happy to be challenged. For your convenience and protection, it would be a good idea to set up a Gatekeeper, to vet any being who tries to communicate through you and only allow beings who work totally for the Light to come into your energy field. You can do all of this purely by intention and it will enable you to work comfortably, knowing that you are protected from any unwanted intrusion. Ask for the name of your Gatekeeper.

Here are the words to a song which I channelled some time ago.

Oh Father Mother God, Great Spirit of the Plains,
Now you and I are one and nothing else remains.
Now you are in my heart, and I Am All That Is,
Now you and I are one, and Love is all that Lives.

Oh friend and lover God, together we will stay,
In peace and joy and love, creating each new day.
Now you are in my heart, and I Am All That Is,
Now you and I are one, and Love is all that Lives.

Clairaudience, Clairsentience and Clairvoyance

Dictionary ~ Clairaudience – *the supposed facility of being able to hear the inaudible.*
No explanation for Clairsentience *but it means, clear feeling or sensing.*
Dictionary ~ Clairvoyance – *the alleged power of perceiving things beyond the natural range of the senses. Keen intuitive understanding.*

Clairaudience comes from the French *clair* meaning clear and *audience,* meaning hearing. It is when you hear with your 'inner ear.' This gift enables you to hear guidance from the other realms. You may also discern the real truth behind what is being said to your face, and you may also be able to occasionally hear someone else's thoughts.

Many people have thought they were going mad because they were hearing voices, but with patience and discernment you can filter out any judgemental or demanding voices, they are not your guides or angels. Divine guidance is always gentle and will suggest rather than command that you do something.
Even though he was deaf, Beethoven heard music in his head!

Clairsentience is when you have a 'feeling' about something. Or sometimes you might describe it as a 'knowing.' I'm sure you can remember situations where you have suddenly just *known* something had happened or was about to happen. It can be particularly strong between loved ones.

Therapists involved with forms of energy healing will sometimes get a pain somewhere in their body. It is not their pain; it is just to show them where they need to focus on their client's body. The pain will disappear when the healing is complete. This is also a form of clairsentience.

Clairvoyance means clear seeing, and some people have exceptional visions and see colours when in a relaxed or meditative state or during a healing procedure. Some clairvoyants have an exceptional gift which they use as their work – giving readings or helping the police for example.

We *all* have these gifts, and usually one or more will be to the fore. Do you know who is calling when the phone rings? How often have you just 'known' something was about to happen, and it did? Have you ever heard your name being called in your head? These are psychic gifts but are not just for a chosen few. We are *all* psychic and can develop further with a little dedication and a lot of practice.

Crystals

Dictionary ~ *a solid, such as quartz, with a regular shape in which plane faces intersect at definite angles.*

Crystals of all kinds and semi precious gemstones are very popular with everyone these days. Whether they be part of jewellery, a 'lucky' stone to carry in your purse or pocket or placed around the house for aesthetic or healing purposes, crystals, rocks and gemstones are to be found everywhere.

They come as clusters, chunks of all sizes, points, wands, carved ornaments and jewellery and tumbled polished gemstones. They are not 'just rocks' as some people may think. They have a very definite energy of their own and each has a different property. Think of them like frozen sunlight or fire. When that energy is released it is very powerful.

Crystals of all kinds can be used for healing the body on all levels. When choosing a crystal or gemstone from a shop, take your time and have the intention to find the perfect stone for your purpose. Handle the stones you feel attracted to and you will know which ones are best for your needs. You may feel a tingle in your hand, or the stone may heat up or feel freezing cold, or you may just not be able to put it down! It feels so right in your hand. Crystals which are given to you as a gift are very special. They have been chosen for you.

It is important to cleanse the crystal as soon as possible to clear it of any negative energies that have been picked up from everyone who has ever handled it from the original miner to the shopkeeper and customers. This can be done simply by holding the stone under running water with the intention that any negativity is removed and returned to the earth. You could also pass the crystal through a flame, or incense smoke or even bury it in the earth for a few days. Under a tree would be a good place. Remember to mark the spot!

Many books on crystals will tell you to programme your crystal for a particular task after you have cleansed it. However, each crystal has its own particular energy, so why would you want to change that? Much better to work intuitively and choose the crystals you *feel* will do the work you require.

Sometimes, a crystal will just disappear for days or even months and then reappear, much to your consternation. They seem to be able to travel to someone who needs them, or sometimes they just need a rest!

A cluster of quartz or amethyst in a room will greatly enhance the atmosphere, while pink rose quartz will spread loving vibrations around. Work intuitively if using crystals for physical healing but placing stones which are the same colour as the chakra in the diseased area will be helpful. If working with quartz or amethyst points, place the points pointing away from the body if you want to draw energy or pain out, and place the points inwards if you want to draw healing energy in.

A very pleasant exercise with a partner, is to hold a piece of rose quartz in front of the forehead, not touching the skin, and move the stone in anticlockwise circles slowly backwards and forwards across the front of the face, moving downwards towards the chin. When you reach the chin, reverse the movements and move upwards in clockwise circles. This gives a lovely 'facial' massage which is calming.

Gem elixirs can be made by placing a clean piece of quartz for example into a jug of spring water, and leaving it overnight. You can drink the water or use it for pets or watering your houseplants. Placing crystals around seedlings and plants will energise them and help them to grow.

A deep blue crystal such as lapis lazuli or sodalite, placed under your pillow, will encourage dreams. Don't keep clear quartz beside your bed as it is too powerful and will keep you awake. Amethyst or rose quartz are gentler and will aid sleep.

If you have an affinity with stones, you will find that there are many books on rocks and minerals available to help you identify your finds.

Devas

Deva is a Sanskrit word which literally means, *'shining one'*. Devas are part of the elemental evolution who have evolved to a stage where they are responsible for looking after large areas of nature like forests or the sea. They will be in charge of other nature spirits and oversee the growth of plant life and trees.

I once had the privilege of talking with a Dutch lady who worked with the nature spirits. She told me that each group of trees, whether it be a small copse or an extensive forest, has its own 'King and Queen' trees. Each tree has a deva in charge of it. If a tree is chopped down or falls, the deva just stays there as it doesn't know anything else. Part of my friend's work was to relocate the deva to a new baby tree. Also, if either the king or queen tree was lost, she bestowed the honour of leadership upon another tree. She spent much time in meditation in woodland communing with the elemental beings.

Sometimes the name, deva is attributed to any of the nature spirits or angels.

Dowsing

Dictionary ~ to *search for underground water, minerals etc. using a divining rod.*

There are a variety of ways of dowsing. You can use twigs, dowsing rods or a pendulum. Traditionally, hazel twigs were used for dowsing or *water witching.* The twigs twitched or moved downwards when held above underground water. No-one knows how it works, it just does! People have been dowsing for thousands of years for water, oil and minerals. Anyone can do it. You just have to have the desire and the patience to practise.

I have only had experience of metal dowsing rods and a variety of pendulums. You can easily make a set of dowsing rods from a metal coat hanger. Cut off the hook and cut through the centre of the horizontal wire and bend to 90 degrees. Hold the short sides in your hands. It is best to insert the short 'handle' ends into plastic tubes so they can move about freely. Old ballpoint pen tubes with the refills removed are ideal, or any piece of short plastic tubing. Stand with your elbows firmly in at your sides and, holding the rods horizontally, focus upon what you are looking for and move slowly forwards until the rods cross.

Here is a fun dowsing exercise you may like to try with some friends.

Have a friend stand some distance away from you. Ask that their thoughts be in 'neutral.' Focus your thoughts on your friend, and ask that the rods cross when you come to the edge of their energy field. Walk steadily towards your friend and mark the position where the rods cross. Now, ask your friend to think of something which makes them very angry or sad. Dowse for the edge of their energy field again, and you will be surprised to find that it has decreased, sometimes quite dramatically. *This shows how our thoughts are affecting our energy all the time. We close down when we are sad or upset.* Mark this spot. Next, ask your friend to think happy thoughts and to beam you lots of love! You will find this time, that the energy field has greatly expanded. If you have a crystal – a piece of clear quartz or any gemstone- ask the friend to hold this while beaming you love and happy thoughts. You will be amazed to see how much further the energy field has grown.

I always enjoy doing this exercise. It not only proves that we have an energy field, and shows how it is affected by our thinking, it shows that crystals amplify energy! Have fun!

Another method of dowsing is by using a pendulum. This can simply be a key on a piece of string or a plumb bob, a charm on a necklace or bracelet chain. There are many pendulums available to buy made of wood, copper or crystal. The ideal length for the chain would be 4-6 inches or 12-15 centimetres. You need to establish what your 'Yes' and 'No' is. Just ask the pendulum to give you a 'yes' and it will possibly circle or swing. Then ask it to give you a 'no' and watch what it does. My pendulum circles clockwise for yes and anticlockwise for no. If it requires more information it swings backwards and forwards. Yours may do quite the opposite. Now, prove to yourself that it works. Say, "My name is (say your name) is this correct?" It should move in your 'yes' way. Now say, "My name is (and state an incorrect name) is this correct?" You should get a 'no' from your pendulum. You are now all set to dowse for whatever you wish.

I mainly use this method in my healing practice for testing for food sensitivities. I work my way down a list of foods and note when the pendulum is telling me that my client is sensitive to a particular item. You can use a pendulum to locate lost things, or to check whether or not you need additional vitamins or minerals. Anything in fact; it works best if you ask questions which require a Yes or No answer. If the answer is somewhere in between or cloudy, the pendulum will hover or swing backwards and forwards.

Apparently, oil companies use dowsers to locate oil and the police use dowsers to help locate missing persons and property, but that is not widely publicised.

You can also dowse with your body. Stand facing North and ask to be shown a 'Yes.' Allow your body to move in whatever way it wants. I start to fall forwards for 'Yes' and backwards for 'No'. There can be all sorts of permutations so don't be surprised if your knees suddenly buckle or you start to sway in a circle! Anything is possible and we are all different.

Dreams

Dictionary ~ *mental activity, usually an imagined series of events, occurring during sleep.*

Dreams have always puzzled mankind and in the past were accepted as a form of Divine Guidance   as in the stories of the Old Testament. I believe that sometimes we do receive answers through the symbology of dreams. It is just yet another way for our Higher Self, Angels or Guides to communicate with us. However, scientists would have us believe that it is just the brain trying to make sense of all the events of the day; so it puts them together in some form of story.

Everyone without exception dreams many times while asleep, but not all dreams are recalled. Occasionally, you may have a particularly vivid dream which you remember forever. Some people dream in colour and others in black and white only. If you find that you *know* when you are dreaming and can control the outcome that is called lucid dreaming.

It is possible to programme yourself to recall your dreams. Settle yourself calmly at bedtime, perhaps with incense in the room or a herb pillow and you might like to place a lapiz lazuli or smoky quartz tumbled stone under your pillow to encourage dreams and psychic awareness. Have a notebook and pen on your bedside table. State the intention that you wish to dream and have recall.

If you waken up during the night, immediately write down some key words relating to what you have just dreamt. Don't try to write a story. The dreams you are most likely to recall are the ones you have just before awakening. Lie still and make yourself remember as much as possible. Once up and about, the dream will vanish rapidly.

Dreams are symbolic, and it doesn't mean for example that you are going to hear of a pregnancy if you dream of a birth. It can mean the start of something new in your life/ new beginnings/ a new job or project for example. People in your dreams are always to do with yourself. If you dream of a man, it has to do with your male aspect and likewise, a woman is your female aspect. Dreaming of your mother could mean that your need to be nurtured more, but don't just go and look up a book for help with the symbolism. You know at some level what the dream means, so ask yourself and you'll get the answer! Sweet dreams.

Ego

Dictionary ~ *the self of an individual person, the conscious subject. One's image of oneself.*

The ego is a belief system in your own mind which you have moulded and identified as being the real you. It outlines boundaries, borders and limits on everything, which gives it the illusion that it is in control and constantly tells you what is right and wrong and how to act, who to judge, how to react in situations etc. The more you obey it, the more it believes itself to be the real you.

Ego shows itself in many guises. We tend to think of someone with 'a lot of ego' as being very full of their own importance, bumptious and big headed, however, the opposite is also a sign of ego being in control. If you continually think that you are not good enough, couldn't cope with a task, are not qualified or experienced enough and so on, that is an aspect of ego creating its illusion of limitation; having you believe that everything is separate from you and outside of yourself.

The ultimate goal is to live without ego; to live in unconditional love - acceptance of everyone, just as they are, with no expectations or judgements; to live in the present moment and to be at one with all. No separation.

Elementals

Dictionary ~ *relating to earth, air, water and fire, considered as elements. A disembodied spirit.*

The elementals are a group of beings that are generally invisible, although their forms of expression surround us through the elements of earth, air, water and fire. Clairvoyants can see them and they can be photographed.

EARTH spirits are called Gnomes. They can be found within rocks, and generally stay close to the ground. They are connected to all stones and minerals, precious gemstones, mountains and all aspects of the geological structure of the planet. Because of their connection to the earth, they can help humans to ground their physical bodies and heighten sensations. They are helpful with gardening.

AIR spirits are called Sylphs. They are volatile and changeable and work through the gases and ethers of the planet. They are particularly sensed through the winds. They sometimes take on a human appearance but only for short periods of time. Because of their connection to air, which is associated with mental activity, they will help humans with inspiration and induce mental clarity.

WATER spirits are known as Undines o'
They are connected with all liquids but the
can be sensed most powerfully beside strer
and the sea. They resemble humans in ap
their size depends upon where they li'
streams and ponds. The mermaids anɑ ...
legend were probably these water spirits. Undinɯ
work with the vital fluids of all water-containing
beings; plants, animals and humans. The watery
aspect is associated with emotion and feelings. They
will protect you while swimming or sailing.

FIRE spirits are the Salamanders. They can be found
in any fire from a tiny match flame to an inferno.
Volcanoes are their natural habitat and they are said to
be the most powerful of the elementals, but the most
illusive to connect with. Said to be lizard-like in shape
but sometimes seen as small balls of light, they are
associated with the human spirit and intuition. They are
purifiers and are very helpful in removing negativity.

To communicate with Elementals, it is necessary to
have a love of nature and a great respect for it. The
elementals communicate telepathically and are very
aware of our feelings and our spiritual awareness.
They will have nothing to do with anyone who
disrespects natural habitats. Try sitting quietly in your
garden or out in nature somewhere, and mentally
invite the nature spirits to commune with you. It may
take more than one attempt, but keep trying and
eventually you will be able to build up a rapport with
them.

It is important when planning to prune trees or
shrubs, to talk to them the day before and warn them
that you are going to cut their branches or stems. This

allows them to withdraw their life force beforehand and the cutting won't be so traumatic for them.

Any time you are going to pick flowers from the garden, ask the flowers which ones would like to be picked. You will then 'know' which flowers are offering themselves to adorn your home or be given as a gift to a friend. Remember to say, "Thank you." Teach this to your children and grandchildren and they will always have respect for growing plants.

Energy

Dictionary ~ intensity *or vitality of action or expression; forcefulness.*

Our energy systems are conscious and intelligent and connected with all other energies in the Universe. They act as a connection between the physical and the metaphysical or spiritual realms. If the energy systems get blocked or damaged in some way, we create illness or disease in our physical bodies (see Chakras).

In fact, we *are* energy. We have an energy field around us (see Auras) which sends out vibes and we are often very aware of other people's energy. I'm sure you can remember a situation when you've walked into a room where the people have just been arguing. You can *feel* the tension in the atmosphere! Sometimes after being in a large crowd, as when you are Christmas shopping or perhaps at a sports stadium, you can feel quite bashed about almost as though you'd been physically beaten. You have been at the mercy of all the different emotions, the frustrations and anger, the depression and concerns as you have been bumping into different energy fields at every turn. If you are normally a healthy and positive person, you will quickly recover your energy. It is essential that you do not allow your energy to be sapped by needy or negative people (see the chapter on Protection).

There are forms of what is called, energy healing. Reiki and Sekhem and Spiritual Healing are but three systems available. Reiki utilises Universal Life Force Energy which is channelled through the crown and comes down the arms and through the hands to the recipient. It flows where it is needed.

People are generally treated lying down so that they can enjoy the relaxation, but can also be treated in a seated position. Healing can be carried out through hands on or 'absent' or 'distant' healing.

Spiritual Healing is similar and the treatments can be done hands on or just off the body. The life force energy used is believed to be Divine, but it is not connected with any religion and no belief is necessary. It can also be sent as 'absent healing'.

Sekhem is a complete vibrational energy system which was known in Ancient Egypt and uses Living Light Energy. This is invoked by the practitioner and brought down through the crown, to the light channel or spine and on into the earth chakra beneath the feet. The energy is immediately focused with an intention which works at the soul level and will always go to any deep underlying cause that needs to be resolved, rather than just addressing the symptoms.

We all return to Source while our physical bodies sleep, so that we can have our energy recharged. Our spirit bodies are attached by a 'silver thread' so we can be back in our bodies in an instant if necessary. We usually have no memory of our nightly journeying.

Etheric

The Etheric is the first level of the subtle bodies which emanate from all living things. It is an exact shape of the person, animal, plant etc and can be perceived with practice (see the chapter on Auras).

Fairies

Dictionary ~ supernatural *being, usually represented in diminutive human form and characterised as having magical powers.* Alternative spelling: faerie or faery.

The fairies and devas are nature spirits which have been presumed to be fictitious, but so many people claim to be able to see and communicate with them that we can accept that they do in fact exist. They often appear as sparkles and small balls of light, but sometimes appear as tiny human-like forms with gossamer wings. The illustrations in the fairytale books down the ages are apparently accurate. Fairies generally are connected with flowers and are the spirits in charge of colouring and growing them.

Celtic folklore is full of stories of both good and bad fairies. Some even steal human babies and replace them with one of their own which is perhaps deformed in some way, according to legend. These babies are called changelings.

For further information on nature spirits, see the chapter on Elementals.

Feng Shui

Feng Shui (pronounced Fung Shwee) literally means Wind and Water. There has been an amazing rise in popularity of Feng Shui in recent years as people are becoming more aware of how energies can affect their lives on all levels. Feng Shui originated in China and is a mixture of ancient wisdom, astrology, folklore and common sense. The Chinese will consult a Feng Shui expert whenever they are building a new block of offices or homes, to check that they are in the most auspicious position for attracting good energy, bringing harmony and prosperity etc.

Externally, the location is very important with the position of hills and water and roads being taken into consideration. Internally, it is concerned with the specific placement of objects and furniture in the office or home which direct good *chi* or energy. Colour is important and direction. Advice is given on the use of mirrors and wind chimes to redirect the energy flow. Clearing out clutter is the first step to balancing the energy in your surroundings, so make that an ongoing task. It allows for the new and fresh things to come into your life. There are many books published on Feng Shui so I will not go into any further details, but suggest that you read up on the subject and then enjoy putting the theory into practice and reaping the benefits.

Flower of Life

The Flower of Life is the name given to a symbol. No one knows exactly how old the symbol is, but there are a number to be found in different locations around the world. There is a flower of life symbol on a granite wall in the middle temple at Abydos in Egypt. It has also been found in Israel, Japan and China.

The sacred geometry of the symbol contains the 'platonic solids' which are the crucial structures that are the building blocks of organic life.

The 'Flower of Life' teachings are to do with sacred geometry and the 17 breath merkaba meditation which will connect you to your Higher Self and strengthen all aspects of your life, as presented by Drunvalo Melchizedek.

To learn about sacred geometry and create your own merkaba vehicle with meditation, contact a Flower of Life facilitator. See www.floweroflife.org

Forgiveness

Dictionary ~ *the act of forgiving or the state of being forgiven.* Forgive ~ *to cease to blame (someone or something) . To grant pardon (for a mistake etc.) To free (someone) from penalty. To free from the obligation of (a debt etc.).*

Forgiveness is the key to moving forward with your life. Many people are unwilling to release themselves from bitterness and hurt. I think the main reason is often because they don't understand that by forgiving someone, they are not *condoning* the act, but they *are* releasing the electrical charge, the pain. By holding on to the anger, hurt or need for revenge, the only person you are hurting is yourself. The other person is totally unaware of your feelings. If you continue to nurture your grievances, you will end up with arthritis or worse. You will literally become 'bitter and twisted.'

We have all been hurt or betrayed or abused at some point in our life; sometimes many times, sometimes through many lives. It is important to picture the perpetrator in your mind and consciously forgive them *from the heart.* You may have to say your forgiveness a number of times until it goes from the head down into the heart. You will know when it has done this as you will feel the relief and may even feel lighter. Forgiveness 'wipes the slate clean'. It is wonderful to know that *there are no karmic debts.*

If the person you feel you haven't been able to forgive until now is still in your life, like a relative or workmate, and you feel unable to say that you forgive them to their face, then write them a letter and hand it over with love.

Most importantly, don't forget to forgive yourself! It doesn't matter how terrible an act you feel you have committed. *Nothing* is unforgivable. God loves you just the way you are and has ALREADY FORGIVEN YOU. The important thing is that you have come through the experience and are now coming from a place of compassion – your heart. Love is the answer. (See the channelled message in the chapter, Angels).

You will find the following affirmations useful. The author is unknown but they are offered for our use by Helen Belot, who reintroduced the Sekhem vibrational energy system to the world.

Repeating each affirmation three times then saying, "so be it" will soon make a difference. Remember, in some cases, you may need to repeat the affirmation many times over a few days until the words get from your head, down into your heart!

Affirmation for Forgiveness and Atonement

**I don't know why you did what you did,
and I don't know why you said what you said,
and I don't know why you are the way you are,
but I accept that's where you need to be now,
and I forgive you and I forgive myself.
I release all anger, bitterness and resentment,
past and present.
And I forgive you and I forgive myself,**

and I release us both in my love.
And so be it.

Atonement is an interesting word.   AT-ONE-MENT.   We are all ONE and so if you hurt another, you are really hurting yourself. Love another, and the love must come back to you.

Forgiveness

I now easily release all resistance
The past has no power over me
I am the only person that thinks in my mind
My mind is powerful
I now choose thoughts that free me
I trust myself to release and let go
I am powerful...and safe...and secure
I am free...I forgive everyone
I forgive myself...
I forgive the past...
And by doing so...I am free
I am free...I am free...

I FORGIVE EVERYONE
I FORGIVE MYSELF
I FORGIVE ALL PAST EXPERIENCES
FORGIVING EVERYONE...FORGIVING MYSELF

I AM FREE......I AM FREE.

Geopathic and Electromagnetic Stress

Geopathic Stress is the term used to describe any illness or discomfort most commonly resulting from the effects of underground minerals, such as boron, underground water or ley lines.

If, for example, your child has difficulty sleeping, it may be caused by one of the above. You could dowse to establish the problem. It may then be solved by simply changing the position of the bed.

Electromagnetic Stress is caused by having a phone, computer, television etc. in your bedroom. Some people are more sensitive to the energies from these electrical items than others. Power lines crossing over your home can also affect your health adversely.

It is thought that cancer can be caused by geopathic or electromagnetic stress. When tests were carried out in Germany years ago, on cancer patients, it was found that each person had geopathic stress in their homes. Either their armchairs or beds were located above some negative energy source. While this doesn't prove that geopathic stress is a cause of cancer, you have to consider the possibility.

If you suspect some geopathic or electromagnetic energy is causing you problems, I suggest you consult an expert who will be able to diagnose and alleviate —

the problem energy by diverting it with copper rods placed at strategic points in your garden, or perhaps the placement of crystals.

Gratitude

Dictionary ~ *a feeling of thankfulness, as for gifts or favours.*

Constantly remembering to give thanks to Source at all times, helps to keep us in an 'attitude of gratitude'. A bit like a blessing, you can be thankful for absolutely everything in your life, from all of your loved ones to things like the bliss of a hot shower, the comfort of your duvet, the beauty of a sunset, your favourite music – the list is endless. We have so much for which to be thankful! You only have to tune in to the news on television or read a newspaper to realise how privileged and rich we are compared with so many others on the planet.

You can turn the most boring task into something worthwhile when you realise that you are able to do it. For a start – many people can't because they are wheelchair bound or hospitalised – and that the act of ironing, or cleaning or painting or whatever will make your part of your world more beautiful or more comfortable.

By being thankful, you are being present and living in the 'now'. You are attracting positive energy and surrounding yourself with love and blessings. When you give thanks to whoever or whatever you imagine God to be, you are attracting even more blessings from the abundant universe. You cannot give out anything without some of it spilling on to yourself.

Guides

Dictionary ~ guide – *to lead the way. To supervise or instruct. To advise or influence.*

We all have guides on the other planes who inspire, impress us with ideas and generally coax us along life's highway and try to keep us on our soul path. This is the contract which we made before we incarnated into this lifetime. Our guides change as our needs differ throughout our life. Once we have had a particular experience or learned a particular lesson, the guide who has been working with us may move on to make way for a new guide to lead us on to bigger and better things.

Our guides can be beings who have never had a life on earth, but usually they are souls who have opted to help us and are often dear relatives who have departed. Many people feel that a parent or grandparent is helping them with decisions or at difficult moments. Some people have angels and ascended masters working with them. At any one time, you will most likely have a team of beings who each assist in a different way. Some will help with emotional challenges, some will help with finances, organising and completing tasks, some will work with healing and so on.

Guides love you unconditionally and will never force you to do anything. Remember, this is the planet of choice and everyone has free will. You will be given opportunities and suggestions and ideas, but in the end, *you* make the decisions and live with the consequences, good or otherwise.

You can communicate with your guides through meditation in the first instance. You may 'see' them in some way – perhaps a Native American or an oriental lady for example. You may be aware of a fragrance or colour when they are active. Talk with them. Ask them to help you. You will get the answers in a variety of ways.

Even if you have never had any apparent proof of their existence, just *know* that they are there. Isn't it wonderful to find that we are not alone after all? We all have Divine help through these beings who were appointed to us – probably some with our knowledge or at our request – before we came down to this Earth School.

Hathors

The Hathors are beings who have gone through a similar evolutionary process to us, and who reside in the etheric of Venus. They are working with us like elder brothers and sisters, to assist us in raising our awareness, so that the Earth can move into the fifth dimension with the least amount of physical upheaval. As they are pure vibration, they have no physical form but can make themselves known to us.

I have been privileged to go on a Hathor workshop where we experimented and played with sound for healing. The Hathors are masters of sound and I subsequently asked them if they would channel sound through my voice for healing purposes, and they do. The strange sounds which emit from my mouth never fail to amaze me; sounds which I could not make normally - sometimes deep and guttural and at other times sweet and sing-song. The energy in the room is tangible and my clients always love the experience and feel physically improved.

At a recent sound healing session with a group of friends, one of them observed that there was a Hathor standing behind each of us with hands on our shoulders. They were swaying in time with the 'music' and obviously enjoying themselves!

For those interested in reading more about The Hathors, I suggest you look at Tom Kenyon's website www.tomkenyon.com and read the book, 'The Hathor Material' by Tom Kenyon and Virginia Essene.

Healing

Dictionary ~ *restoring or being restored to health.*

The physical body is constantly healing and repairing cells and tissue with no conscious effort on your part. It is always striving towards good health. You can greatly assist this process by doing the following:

Eat a varied diet of fresh food, with plentiful fruit and vegetables. Try to buy organic produce where possible and no GM food. Remember, your body can't possibly be anything other than what you put into it. Eat junk food each day and your body will resemble a scrapyard in the long run!

Drink lots of water – at least 6 – 8 glasses a day and more if you are doing energy work.

Get adequate sleep. Some people now feel that they need only a few hours of sleep. That makes more time for the next thing.

Meditate. Taking even just a few minutes in the day to sit quietly and still your thoughts will reduce blood pressure and allow you to become centred and calmer.

Exercise in some way which you enjoy. Dance, run, play sport or simply walk and look at the scenery around you. Whatever you do, get *moving.*

Have some **relaxation** time. Listen to music, do a crossword or Sudoku, read, play an instrument, paint, whatever...but just get creative sometimes.

Do what you can to prevent dis-ease. Enjoy a regular massage or have Bowen or Reflexology treatments for example. Take a good multivitamin and mineral combination to combat the lack of nutrients in our soil nowadays, and also the polluted air and the chemicals we ingest. Maintain a positive outlook and an attitude of gratitude!

Your mental state greatly affects your physical body. By changing your negative thoughts and words to positive, you will give your brain life enhancing instructions. Every time you change any limiting belief within yourself, any thought that makes you feel belittled, you improve. Release any guilt that you are holding and forgive everyone, and especially yourself.

Forms of spiritual healing such as Reiki, Sekhem or Angel healing can bring about miracles when the combination of spiritual, physical and mental healing combine with your willingness to release anything which no longer serves your Higher Purpose.

Sometimes people are called Healers, but remember that they don't do the healing, that is done by the recipient of the healing energy which they are channelling.

Higher Self

The Higher Self or Sacred Self as some people prefer to call it is the part of you which is your God connection; the part of you which can see the bigger picture and knows exactly what you need.

Before you came into this incarnation, you would have planned what you wished to experience with your Higher Self. Some things are set in stone and *must* be experienced, but as this is a planet of free will, sometimes we will wander away from the path we'd planned and our Higher Self, plus our Guides, will gently but firmly nudge us back on course.

It is helpful from time to time to meet with your Higher Self in meditation to discuss any challenge you may be facing and to ask for clarity and guidance.

I Ching

Dictionary ~ *an ancient Chinese book of divination and a source of Confucian and Taoist philosophy.*

The I Ching or 'Book of Changes' or, to give it its most accurately translated title, the 'Classic of Changes', is the oldest of the Chinese classics. It describes an ancient system of philosophy which focuses on the balance of opposites, the evolution of events as a process and the acceptance of the inevitability of change.

Many people believe that it portrays the wisdom and philosophy of Ancient China, but in the West it is regarded as a means of divination: an oracle. There are 64 abstract line arrangements called hexagrams, each of which represents a state, a process or a change. The hexagrams are cast and then interpreted.

Further information can be found on the internet or in any bookshop.

Indigos

Indigo children are so called because of the predominance of the colour indigo in their auras. They are a particular group of souls who incarnated from 1978 onwards with a definite purpose in the near future.

Possible indications that you may be or have an indigo are that they are usually gifted in some way, perhaps musically or artistically; they are extremely headstrong and know what they want. They can sometimes be diagnosed as ADHD or ADD. They get bored easily as they know that a lot of the stuff they are getting in school will not be what they require for their work. They have deep compassion for animals and nature in general and a desire to help the world. Some indigos find it difficult to sleep and may have nightmares or fear of sleeping. They can be prone to depression and can become addicted to harmful substances.

If you feel you may have an indigo child, it is important to channel their extra energy into creative pursuits otherwise they will end up bored and become disruptive and surly. Anything to do with art, music, dance, cookery or sports would be suitable. The child will have a leaning towards a particular activity. While this is true of any child, it is vital that the indigo does not end up on Ritalin or some such drug, as this dulls their memory of why they are here as well as making them more likely to become dependent on addictive substances.

It is important also that the indigo has a highly nutritious diet with the appropriate vitamins and minerals. A diet of junk food and carbonated drinks will quickly cause hyperactivity which could lead to a misdiagnosis of ADHD.

A book which you may find helpful is, *'The Care and Feeding of Indigo Children' by* Doreen Virtue.

The next wave of children to come in were the Crystal Children. It is reassuring to know that there are so many highly evolved souls who are willing to come to Earth in these times to bring about a peaceful existence in the future.

Initiation

Dictionary ~ initiation - *the* ceremony, often secret, initiating new members into an organization.

Initiations have been used by all manner of organisations and societies down through the ages. They were part of the learning curve of students in the Mystery Schools of Ancient Egypt, acknowledging their passage from one level to another.

Secret societies, like the Masons, have always been known to hold initiations, and even young boys will invent a ritual involving solemn promises and perhaps weird actions, which everyone has to go through to become a member of their gang or club. They may call this a form of initiation but it is really a ritual.

In Reiki healing, there is something called an attunement, which enables the recipient to channel the healing energy. An attunement is an adjustment of the energy field to allow the Universal Life Force Energy to come through. It's a bit like tuning in a radio to a new station, and can be repeated over and over again.

An initiation, on the other hand, is introducing something new into the energy field. It is only done once and holds for all time. The energy system, Sekhem, is a good example of this. The recipient is initiated into the energy and this enables them to channel the Living Light Energy of Sekhem. They only need to have a repeat initiation if they have an attunement or initiation to energy of lesser vibration than Sekhem. You are only as good as your last initiation. Each one that you have overwrites the previous one.

Inner Child

When you were a child, you quickly learned the behaviour which was acceptable. Throwing a tantrum and screaming and kicking are ok when you are aged two or three, but you quickly realise that the anger has to be suppressed in order to fit in socially and also probably to get what you want. There are also times when you will have felt jealousy, sadness and even great grief or fear as a child. These emotions are still trapped within and we all have an Inner Child and an Inner Adolescent who cry out for help and attention from time to time.

You may have experienced a time in your life when you have been overcome by a sudden jealousy perhaps, which has come out of nowhere and taken you by surprise. Or it could be a fear of the dark, or of water. This could be your Inner Child reacting, not the adult that you are now. It is a good idea to take the time to do a meditation to reach your Inner Child and ask what they need from you. You may be surprised at their request. They may need hugs and comforting or want you to play with them. Just visualise holding your Inner Child or playing on the swings together, or brushing their hair or whatever comes up for you. Make a point of visiting with your Inner Child on a regular basis until they are completely reassured and feeling safe. You will find that you will be more balanced emotionally as a result.

Intuition

Dictionary ~ knowledge *or belief obtained neither by reason or perception. Instinctive knowledge or belief. A hunch or unjustified belief.*

How many times have you just *known* something? Even simple things like knowing who is phoning when the phone rings. This is your intuition working. Some people call it your sixth sense.

Others will talk about having a 'gut feeling' about something. It is important to follow those feelings when they occur. Just by instinctively taking a different route home, you may discover that you avoided an accident or traffic jam. If you feel strongly that you have to tell someone something, just do it, even though you might feel a little self conscious about it. You will probably find that the message or few words that you have relayed are very pertinent to them.

Our instinctual knowledge or intuition is often guidance from our unseen spiritual helpers. The more you follow your intuition, the more often it will be used. There are no such things as 'coincidences'. Everything that happens has a meaning or message for you. Nothing is by chance!

Journal

Dictionary ~ journal - a book in which a daily record of happenings is kept.

If you aren't already keeping a journal, start one straight away! You can use anything from an old jotter to a beautiful notebook, but just get writing. You don't have to enter something every day, like a diary, unless you choose to. Note down all the exciting happenings in your life. (*What* exciting happenings? I hear you ask); well, just start to pay attention to all the little things from day to day. You might like to write down affirmations that you are saying. It's also a good idea to write down some of your blessings each day. It keeps you centred and in a place of humility. Record the happenings at any workshops you attend; your dreams; the state of your health.

I started to keep a journal a number of years ago when I first set out on this path of self discovery. I find it amazing and entertaining to read again all the things which I've done and experienced. I can see how I have grown in understanding along the way. To give you an example, when I first learned to do healing work, I recorded every detail of the many challenging treatments I did involving psychic surgery, colour or sound. I was completely enthralled by anything 'unusual' or 'coincidental'. In more recent times, I noticed that I rarely mention those things – not because I no longer experience them, quite the contrary, because they are now so normal for me. I accept having guidance, working with angels, moving entities, working with sound and crystals all in a day's work.

Kabbalah

Dictionary ~ cabbala, cabala, Kabbala, or kabala – an ancient Jewish mystical tradition.

Although the Kabbalah is an ancient Jewish tradition, non-Jews can easily relate to it and benefit from the teachings.

It is taught that everything in the universe is an expression of God, so there is no difference between sacred and secular life. Every thought, feeling or action should be an expression of the conscious awareness of the Divine in all things.

There are three methods of achieving and maintaining this state. They are:

Action – Which can be in the form of a daily routine or ritual that is a sincere act of worship of God.

Devotion – Which could include looking after someone lovingly, or being grateful and counting your blessings, or simply praying.

Contemplation – Which involves reflection or meditation on spiritual and world matters.

Sincerely following the above methods without ego will ultimately lead to the development of greater insight and intuition and a closer relationship with the Divine.

The Tree of Life is something which was devised so that people could better understand the descent of the Divine. Ten spheres representing the sephiroth (attributes of God) are arranged upon three pillars with interconnecting paths.

They consist of Keter (the Crown), Chokhmah (wisdom), Binah (understanding), Chesed (mercy), Guevara (strength, judgement), Tiferet (glory, beauty), Netzach (victory), Hod (majesty), Yesod (foundation) and Malkhut (sovereignty or the Kingdom). The Ten Sephiroth contain both masculine and feminine qualities.

I have just touched on a tiny part of the teachings of the Kabbalah here and if you are serious about studying it, I suggest you find a teacher.

When I was on the Angels 2000 week at Findhorn, one of the speakers was unable to attend due to illness and it was decided to build a gigantic Tree of Life which covered the central part of the floor of the main hall. The artists concerned stayed up all night long to create a beautiful picture of a tree depicting the moon and stars and many birds, on large sheets of paper. It was a work of art.

The audience was then invited into the hall which was darkened. A pianist was playing sweet music and we were each given a small candle to place wherever we chose on the picture of the tree on the floor. No-one spoke, the atmosphere was reverent yet electric. Each person stepped up in turn, lit their candle, spent a few moments in contemplation and then placed their light on the tree. The memory of over 300 candles lighting up that beautiful Tree of Life will remain with me always.

Karma

Dictionary ~ *Hinduism, Buddhism. The principle of retributive justice determining a person's state of life and the state of his reincarnations as the effect of his past deeds. Destiny or fate.*

Karma simply means, 'what goes around, comes around' or 'as you sow, so shall you reap'. We forever have to deal with the consequences of our actions. If our actions have been kind and well meant, we will receive some lovely surprises in our day to day lives; perhaps some unexpected money, friends offering us a holiday, a beautiful gift for example. We never know when we are going to reap the benefits or otherwise, of our deeds. Up until this lifetime, karma could be carried forward into future lives, so if you didn't handle something wisely, you could always have another chance to do things differently in another lifetime.

However, this is the lifetime that counts. Many of us have opted to clear all our accrued karma this time around, and to raise our vibration. This is probably a reason why there are so many problems within families and countries. Karmic debts are becoming due and there is not much time left to settle them.

Before we were born, we chose our parents, physical disposition, and life experiences, so we only have ourselves to blame if we find ourselves in challenging circumstances. However, you only carry karma until you have learnt your lesson. Don't keep repeating past mistakes; free yourself with awareness and love.

If you find that you never seem to be able to 'get away with anything', it is probably because you have cancelled all of your karmic debts and are living in instant karma. If you are judgemental or speak angrily, you will find that the same treatment will be dished out to you within a few hours!

Love and kindness have a way of cancelling karma. Forgiveness and compassion will heal all relationship difficulties. If you still feel that there is a situation which you can't solve yourself, petition God, through the Lords of Karma for divine dispensation, to release your karma.

Kundalini

Kundalini is a Sanskrit word meaning: *'coiled up' or 'coiling like a snake'*. Some other interpretations suggest it means, *'serpent power'*. The cadeuseus symbol used in the medical and complementary therapy world, of a staff with two coiled snakes, is thought to be an ancient representation of Kundalini physiology.

In Western terms, the Kundalini energy is stored at the root chakra and when released, it uncoils up the spine awakening and empowering the other chakras as it travels. If some of the lower chakras are blocked, then there is still work for us to do to unblock them. There is no benefit in having the higher chakras opened and thinking that you are spiritually advanced if the lower ones are still undeveloped. All of the chakras are of equal importance in your development.

Kundalini is mainly associated with Hinduism. There is a form of Kundalini Yoga which incorporates meditational and breathing practices and concentrates on the spine and endocrine system.

Labyrinth

Dictionary ~ a *mazelike network of tunnels, chambers or paths, either natural or manmade.*

A labyrinth differs from a maze in that it is one continuous path which leads to the centre and then returns to the entrance again. The most famous labyrinth is in Chartres Cathedral in France.

The type most commonly made today is the classic or seven circuit labyrinth. It has a Christian background as the cross is the central starting point for constructing the labyrinth.

My first experience of 'Walking the Labyrinth' was a few years ago when a friend constructed a beautiful labyrinth of smooth, white stones, gemstones and nightlights. The effect was very reverent and spiritual and I found the process quite thought-provoking and moving.

There is no right or wrong way to walk a labyrinth, but here are some guidelines.

1. Pause and centre yourself. Focus your thoughts.
2. Experience fully whatever feelings arise during your walk into the centre. Pause there for as long as you choose, then return to the exit.

3. Reflect upon your feelings and thoughts and write your experiences in your journal.

I have constructed two labyrinths with members of my night class which was fun and they enjoyed the experience. We used shells, fir cones, crystals, nightlights, flowers and twigs. This was to make it easier for us to put together as stones would have been prohibitively heavy to carry to an evening class! It is a different experience each time the labyrinth is walked. You can also have a small printed version which you can 'walk' with your finger when feeling stressed.

Leylines

Dictionary ~ a line joining two prominent points in the landscape, thought to be the line of a prehistoric track.

Ancient sites all over the country can be joined up on a map with a ruler. Some think that these lines are the tracks commonly used by the people of the time, but as some of the lines go straight up steep mountains, that is probably not completely correct. Some people believe that the ley lines have special energy and that where they cross, the energy is greatly magnified. The pre-reformation churches and cathedrals were built upon crossed ley lines. It would seem that at one time we were able to tune in to these energy lines and utilise them, but that ability has been lost over the generations. Nowadays there is a renewed interest in returning to living close to nature and following our intuition.

One way to connect with ley lines is to dowse for them (see the chapters on *Dowsing* and *Geopathic* and *Electromagnetic Stress)*.

Standing stones across the country are apparently connecting up the energy of the ley lines criss-crossing the land. Birds and animals follow energy lines when migrating. The aboriginals in Australia call ley lines, song lines.

Mandala

Dictionary ~ Any *of various designs, sometimes symbolising the universe, usually circular.*

I was given a book of Mandalas for Meditation which is in effect, a colouring book for grown-ups. It turned out to be one of the most relaxing and rewarding of experiences to sit down and lose myself in the picture on which I was working. Each one is in the form of a circle and therefore you are either starting at the centre and colouring outwards to the edges, or working inwards from the outer areas. It is a way of focusing and centring yourself while remembering to be as a child, learning the rules, keeping within the lines, yet having the freedom of choice of colours. Even if hundreds of people were to colour in the same page, no two would be exactly the same. That is what makes the colouring of mandalas so interesting. I thoroughly recommend it.

Much of the stuff of life is in the form of a mandala: a circle. Each cell has its nucleus, which remains resting at the centre most of the time, and although individual cell shapes may vary, the principle of controlling from the centre is the same in each. Everything revolves from the centre.

A drop of water can be considered to be circular, and it contains a whole microcosm of life in just one tiny drop.

Millions of water mandalas create the beauty of a rainbow. Returning to our bodies, we are composed of millions of mandalas too. Our cells and atoms, our veins and ducts, fingerprints and eyes are just a few. Those who can see chakras, draw them as mandala flower shapes.

Everywhere in nature there are mandalas. Slice a fruit or onion and there is a mandala. Cut through a tree trunk, look into a rose, look up at the sky through a tree; everywhere, mandalas.

If you'd like to create a mandala yourself you could make a native american-style dream catcher. It is very therapeutic and it has been said that every menopausal woman should make her own dreamcatcher! It is a hoop of wood (an embroidery ring is ideal) through which you loop wool or thread to form what looks a bit like a spider's web. Beads or crystals can be included and it is then decorated with feathers or items of your choice. There are instructions following.

Dreamcatcher - Materials
- **Strong thread**
- **Metal or wooden ring of any size (a ring used for holding embroidery cloth would be ideal)**
- **Suede lacing, long narrow strip of material or wool**
- **Beads, crystals, feathers**

Dreamcatcher
How to make it:
1. Knot one end of the suede lacing or wool on the ring. Make sure to leave four or five inches or 12 centimetres of lacing to hang the dreamcatcher before winding the suede tightly around the ring until it is entirely covered.

2. Tie off the suede and knot the two remaining ends together to form a loop to hang the dreamcatcher on.

3. Cut off a long length of thread. Tie one end to the top of the ring.

4. Now it gets a little tricky. The webbing is made up of a net of 'half hitch' knots. To make the first knot, loop the thread over the hoop towards the back then bring the thread to the front again by pulling it up through the hole you've made between it and the hoop. Make sure to keep the thread pulled taut.

5. Going around the hoop, keep making these knots at seven or eight evenly spaced points.

6. When you get back to the top of the hoop, start the next round by making knots on the loops of thread from the first round.

7. Thread a bead into the webbing whenever you like.

8. You should have a small hole left in the centre when you finish the webbing. Tie a double knot and cut the rest of the thread off.

9. To make feather tassels to hang off the dreamcatcher, cut a few lengths of suede or wool and tie them to the bottom of the dreamcatcher.

10. Push a few beads onto each piece of suede lacing or wool and tie knots to make sure they don't move. Push the ends of the feathers through the beads to complete your dreamcatcher.

Another way of creating a mandala is simply to relax into a meditative state and while listening to some beautiful music or chant, draw and colour whatever images come to you. Sometimes, something which needs to be brought to your attention to be released may appear in your pictures. You could also try asking a question before you start, and then see what comes to you in image form. It's a bit like dreaming...the answers will be in symbolic form.

Manifesting

Dictionary ~ Manifestation – *the act of demonstrating; an indication or sign; the materialisation of.*

You are creating your future with every thought that you think. Think about that one again...

You are creating your future with every thought that you think!

What kind of future do you desire? Are your thoughts generally positive and happy or are you constantly thinking of all the bad things that could happen to you? We are bombarded with negativity by the media and it would be easy to think that we are living in a terrible world where we are constantly under threat by terrorists and other such horrors.

This is not necessarily the case. We live in an ever-expanding universe with an unlimited supply of everything we could ever imagine. Imagining what we want is the key.

You first of all **think** of something, or it could be that you ask for it, or pray for it. It is then available for you. All your prayers are always answered instantly. It may not seem like that to you, of course, because you have not allowed them to manifest. For example, if you are feeling ill and have asked to be well again, that thought has created the wellness, but you have kept your thoughts on your pain or feelings of being unwell, and the *lack* of wellness is what you are concentrating on for most of the time. It follows then that the universe gives you more of the illness as that is what you are putting out with your thoughts and probably your talk. You need to focus on the *feeling* of being completely well again and imagine that often and then wellness will come to you instead of the *lack* of it.

You attract in this life what you focus on. You can have whatever you choose. A satisfying career, a loving partner, money, good health, peace and so on will materialise when you concentrate your thoughts and feelings on what you desire (and not the lack of it).

Each morning when you awaken, give thanks for another day and ask that it be filled with love and happy things. If you are going on a car journey, ask that it be smooth and uneventful and that you arrive at your destination on time. You can be practising your 'attitude of gratitude' as you drive and give thanks for the sunshine (or the rain) and the trees, and your warm car and the way it is so reliable etc. At each step of your day, consciously plan how you want it to be. Draw towards you only that which you desire and do not focus on anything else.

Stop reading the papers and watching the news if this fills you with fear for the future. **You** can change things by creating your own happy life filled with wonderful things and loving relationships and this will in turn have a ripple effect on everyone with whom you come into contact.

Meditation

Dictionary ~ *reflection, contemplation of spiritual matters.*

Meditating can be one of the most challenging aspects of leading a spiritual life. We are constantly being told to 'go within', 'sit in the stillness', 'allow your mind to go blank!' Well, to the newcomer to meditating, this can all seem a bit impossible. What is meant by 'going within?' How can you get your mind to go blank and sit in the stillness, when as soon as you try to do that, your thoughts go into overdrive?

Be reassured, we have all been there and most of us still have times when the 'chattering monkey' thoughts can crowd in. However, here are hopefully some helpful techniques for you to try until you find your own particularly effective way of reaching a meditative state.

Firstly, it is important to be able to relax completely. Choose a place to sit, where you will not be disturbed. This may be in your garden, or more usually, in a room in your home. Tell the family that you must not be disturbed, switch off the phone or do whatever you need to do to have peace. It's a good idea to meditate in the same place each time. You may like to light a candle or have some incense or fragrant oils burning, but this is not essential, just enjoyable. It helps to create a peaceful ambiance.

It is probably better to sit upright either in a chair or on a low stool or cushion, rather than to lie down, as you will tend to fall asleep then.

Start to relax your body, bit by bit. You can start at your head and work down or start at your feet and work up, it doesn't matter. Take your time and become aware of each part of your body in turn, and then allow it to relax. Once you have completed this, scan through your body with your inner knowing, and if you still have some tension or pain anywhere, breathe into it, and then allow it to be released down through your feet into the earth. Now you are relaxed and comfortable.

A good way to help find stillness is to 'watch' your breath. Just take your awareness to your breathing and watch the air coming in through your nose, going down into your lungs and coming out again. Don't try to change your breathing, just observe it. If you find that other thoughts come into your mind, that's okay. Just let them go and continue to observe your breath. Do this for a few minutes only, the first time, and gradually increase the time you spend each day. By following the same ritual, your brain and body will quickly go into relaxed mode. When you want to, bring your awareness back into your body, wiggle your fingers and toes, increase your inhalation and exhalation and open your eyes, feeling relaxed and refreshed. It is always a good idea to ground yourself by imagining roots growing downwards into the earth from the soles of your feet. Should you at any time feel 'spacey' or dizzy after a meditation, then stamp your feet on the ground and go and have a drink of water and something to eat. Food will always earth you. (My friends and I decided that carrot cake must be the best thing to earth you as carrots are root vegetables!).

Another good way of stopping that 'monkey chatter' is to give your brain something to concentrate on by repeating a Mantra. A mantra is just any word which you continually repeat. I suggest words like RE-LAX, SE-RENE, TRAN-QUIL which can be repeated like this...breathe in while saying, "RE" then breathe out while saying, "LAX". Sit with your eyes closed repeating the words aloud on your breath and after a few minutes, change it to a whisper, and then after another few minutes, say the word silently in your head. You'll find that this will help you to become very calm and relaxed.

Chanting is another way of meditating which I find particularly helpful. You can simply repeat the OM or AAUUMMMMM, over and over. Sacred chants like, OM MANI PADME HUM, of OM NA MA SHIVAYA are readily available as beautiful recordings on CD, and are great to sing along with. It focuses the mind and brings you into your centre. Wonderful to do with a group of people and the vibration can be felt once you have stopped chanting and just sit in the silence together.

Deep healing can occur whenever the physical body relaxes totally and guided visualisations are very helpful for this. There are many tapes, CD's and books containing guided visualisations and they are most effective. However, you can visualise a scene yourself without having someone read to you or listening to a CD. Just relax down...then imagine yourself going through a doorway and into the scenery of your choice. It could be a beautiful walled garden, a seashore, a forest, a mountainside or someplace else. Just go to somewhere that you love, and experience it with all of your senses. Feel the sunshine or breeze on your skin, smell the salt air/ flowers/leaf mould etc, listen to the sound of the birds/water/insects or complete silence. Look closely at the entire scene around you. Taste some fruit or drink some water if appropriate.

Spend as long as you like in your special place, knowing that you can return there whenever you choose. Sometimes, another being may join you. It could be your Higher Self or a Guide or Angel. Take time to sit or walk with them and be aware of any information they may be imparting to you.

Bring yourself back to your room as before, and ground yourself.

"That's all very well, but I can't visualise" I hear you say! Well, everyone can visualise. It just means to imagine. Close your eyes and picture your front door. Did you do that? Of course, you did. Everyone can picture their own front door in their mind. Well, following a visualisation is just the same. Here are some other things for you to try:

Close your eyes and try to think of the following:

- A pen slowly writing you name on paper
- Shapes – a green triangle, a blue circle, a yellow square, a red cross
- A tulip

To focus on the sensation of touch, imagine:

- Stroking a cat or dog

- Running your fingers over the bark of a tree
- Rolling an orange in your hands and feeling its dimpled texture

Imagine the taste and texture of:

- Chocolate
- Lemon
- Olives

Try to conjure up the following:

- The smell of freshly baked bread
- Woodsmoke
- Ground coffee

In your mind's ear, listen to:

- The drone of a bee
- Waves breaking on the seashore
- The sound of a gong, very gradually fading into the distance.

How did you do? I'm sure you managed to imagine some if not all of the things.

Here is a guided visualisation which can help your to see the bigger picture if you have a problem and can assist you in feeling part of the Oneness.

Raindrops

First of all, Relax down...then...

Imagine yourself becoming very small and go down into your heart space...

In front of you there is a beautiful, wooden door with pictures of birds and flowers and leaves carved in it.........Open the door, and step through into a wonderful, yet familiar landscape. In front of you is a lake, with hills in the distance and a shingle shore just ahead. The air is fresh and you can hear the birds, and the insects busying around.....The sky begins to cloud over and suddenly large droplets of rain fall down all around you.........become aware of the raindrops..........*become* a *raindrop*......

Imagine what it is like to be a glistening, droplet of water.........free....pure ....you know that you are just one of millions, but you are a perfect droplet of clear water.

Suddenly, you splash into the lake............and everything changes............You now have an awareness of the whole lake.........you know every inch of the bottom, every stone and reed, every fish and water snail.........You know every part of the shoreline.........every tiny pebble...each grain of sand.....every blade of grass and tree root......you can see the sky above, and there is not one single part of the lake that you do not know.......you are the *whole lake*..........The drops of water are so integrated with each other, that the drops comprise the entirety of the lake or the lake's unified field..........together, they comprise the whole reality......there are no parts of the lake which are not an aspect of you...

Retaining this feeling of knowing and seeing the bigger picture, bring yourself back to the carved wooden door and once again, enter into your heart space.

Increase your inhalation and exhalation and gradually bring yourself back. Be aware of the roots growing down from the soles of your feet into the earth, and gradually open your eyes a little bit at a time, until you are back to full awareness holding on to that Higher perspective.

Some people find that they can reach a meditative state quickly by sitting quietly and staring at a candle, or flower or a favourite crystal or gemstone. Examine every inch of your chosen aid. Close your eyes and 'see' the image inside your head. When it fades, just open your eyes again and repeat the process for as long as you require. You could listen to music and allow images to form in your head. You could then put them down on paper in the form of a mandala (see chapter on Mandalas) and use coloured pencils to complete your picture.

As you can see, there are many ways of being meditative, which don't require you to sit in the lotus position and chant Om for hours! Just trying to be in the present moment at all times, focusing on the task in hand with gratitude and appreciation is a form of meditation in itself.

Namaste

I honour the place in you in which the entire
universe dwells.
I honour the place in you which is of love,
of truth, of light and peace.
When you are in that place in you,
and I am in that place in me,
we are one.

Numerology

Dictionary ~ *the study of numbers, such as the figures in a birth date, and of their supposed influence on human affairs.*

Numerology was introduced to us in the West by the Greek philosopher, Pythagoras of Samos (582-507 B.C.) It has its roots in the ancient teachings of India and Egypt and some of the symbology is found in the Bible and in the Jewish Kabbalah.

By checking out your name and date of birth in numerology, you will learn about your personal qualities which will allow you to live in a more balanced way and not just become a victim of fate.

1	2	3	4	5	6	7	8	9
A	B	C	D	E	F	G	H	I
J	K	L	M	N	O	P	Q	R
S	T	U	V	W	X	Y	Z	

To work out your Name number, add all the numbers relating to the letters in your name together and reduce them to a single number.

e.g. John Smith
685 + 14928
20   +   24 = 44 = 8

John Smith's Name number is 8

To work out your Birthpath number, add together all the numbers in your birth date.

e.g. Matthew's birth date is 29/11/1999

$2 + 9 + 1 + 1 + 1 + 9 + 9 + 9 = 41 = 5$

Matthew's Birthpath number is 5

There are many more calculations which you can do, and if you are interested then there is much to be had on the internet and many good books on the subject.

It is interesting to work out your Name number on the full name you were given at birth and then work out the number for the name you are using now. Do you shorten your given name like, Pat or Liz or Matt? When you write your signature, do you use your forename as well or just the initial?

It's worth thinking about; because that is the vibration you are sending out to the world all the time.

Number One
Positive – Courage, originality, leadership ability, the promotion of fortitude and honesty. Can be strong willed and ambitious. Have a desire to be first in all things – literally number one. They can be demanding and commanding, and often witty, charming and dignified; quick decision makers who are looked to for guidance. Robust, energetic and healthy.

Negative – Self-centredness, brash and assertive manner to hide insecurities, rarely ask others help, passive, stubborn.

Number Two
Positive – Peace, partnership, co-operation, modesty, tact, good listener. Highly adaptable and flexible. Holds the belief that good will always triumph over evil.

Negative – Oversensitive, so can be easily hurt. When thwarted, can be cunning or scheming. Needs constant assurance and encouragement.

Number Three
Positive – Creative, joyful, imaginative. Blessed with optimism and love to socialise. They are good and loyal friends.

Negative – Talk too much while saying very little, self centred, scattered and undisciplined.

Number Four
Positive - Practical, reliable, hard working, loyal and dedicated. They carry out their work seriously and honestly.

Negative – Tendency to be rigid and fixed in their attitudes. Don't like sudden change. They like routine and are very organised. Can be very resentful to those who they perceive as getting more than they deserve.

Number Five
Positive - Freedom, love of adventure, energy, interest in spirituality, curiosity, sensuality. They are carefree and witty with enthusiasm for life.

Negative – Careless disregard for rules. Difficulty in staying attached to people or places for any length of time. Flirtatious and fickle. Impatient with slow moving situations.

Number Six
Positive - Sympathetic and considerate. They like

service, domesticity and are generous and empathetic. They like emotional harmony. Will sacrifice their own interests for others.

Negative - Susceptible to other people's feelings and moods, which causes them discouragement, insecurity and anxiety. Can be petty over trivial matters and overbearing.

Number Seven

Positive - Thirst for knowledge and a seeker of truth. Dignified and poised. Eloquent and charming. Concerned with spirituality and the higher truths and mysteries of the universe.

Negative – Often appear as detached or indifferent. Can make impulsive statements which they later regret. Can be cynical and untrusting.

Number Eight

Positive - Leadership and success. Efficient and organised they are at home in the competitive world. Self disciplined and ambitious.

Negative – Tendency to overwork leaving little time for personal matters. Can be ruthless and overly suspicious of others. Reluctant to show tenderness lest it be taken for weakness.

Number Nine

Positive - Compassion, generosity, tolerance. Artistic, spiritual and mystical they inspire others through their leadership. Nines have come to serve and will do anything for their loved ones. Kind and loving, they also crave affection and understanding.

Negative - Prone to depression and states of melancholy. Emotionally impressionable and can be taken advantage of easily.

OM

OM is supposedly the sound which is made when all the sounds in the world are put together. It is used as a mantra while meditating and can be sounded as AUM exaggerating the aaaaa..auu...mmmm sound or just as OM. It is extremely powerful.

If you ever find yourself in fear or extreme difficulty, start to om. Even if you can only do it silently or whisper it, continue until you get your strength and voice back.

Om-ing together in a group is a wonderful, meditational experience. Vary when each of you starts, so that you are not all taking a breath at the same time, and the sound just flows on and on.

Prayer

Dictionary ~ *a personal communication or petition addressed to a deity, especially in the form of supplication, adoration, praise, contrition, or thanksgiving.*

Some people feel unable to pray because they think they don't know how to do it, but there is no special way to pray other than speaking from the heart. Talking with God is just like talking to a close friend. Tell Him/Her everything. God loves to hear of your happiness as well as being ever open to your requests.

Some will feel that they are more reverent if they are kneeling, or that prayers are only to be said in church. However, it may be simpler to think of prayer as just the same as a thought. You are part of God, there is no separation, so every thought, wish, dream or desire is already known to your Creator who will always answer your prayers for your highest good. Just like a good parent with their child, it will not always be instant gratification or in the way that you expect it.

If there is something troubling you, 'Let go and let God'. Just explain everything to God and ask for help, then let it go. There is no sense in keeping repeating your prayer. It would then mean that you didn't believe that God would help in the first place, so you've had to ask again! Just be patient, maintaining an attitude of gratitude, and all will be resolved, sometimes in the most amazing ways.

Protection

Dictionary ~ *defence from trouble or harm.*

The more spiritually aware you become and the finer your vibration, the brighter your light shines. There must always be balance in this universe, so that means you will attract more of the darkness. Let's call them 'the opposition.' There is no need to be fearful – that would be success for the opposition – just take sensible precautions. You protect your home and contents and also your car with insurance, in the hope that you will never need it, but if you do, there will be sufficient cash and support to take care of the situation.

It is the same with your 'bodies.' Every day, make sure that you surround yourself with protection of some kind. It can be as simple as imagining white light swirling around you, or a bubble which moves with you, to repeating an affirmation which you are comfortable with. You may like to put a sacred symbol around yourself, or put yourself in a pyramid. Always make sure that you are not only keeping out the darkness but allowing that which is of love and light to enter your energy field. Perhaps putting on your protection while having your morning shower would be a good way of making it part of your routine.

Here is a little verse which I use each day for protection:-

In the name of God, I call forth my mighty I Am presence, to access the Gold Ray of Christ for my total protection.

Repeat this three times, then say – So be it.

You could equally call upon Archangel Michael to surround you in his blue cloak of protection or any other deity or god/goddess that you feel drawn to.

Always remember that light floods into a darkened room - the darkness cannot come out! Even the light from a tiny match will light up the darkness. We have the power in the dark and in the light.

Psychic Attack

A psychic attack can happen when you are weakened in some way, perhaps by illness, drugs or alcohol, so it is wise to *always* protect yourself. Even then, sometimes jealousy or a similar emotion can infiltrate your energy field and make you feel ill. You may have a sudden headache for no apparent reason, or feel that your aura has been 'buzzed.' Fear will only make things worse, so be aware of that.

A simple remedy is to mentally surround yourself with mirrors – in front, behind, above and below. You could put yourself into a mirrored egg shape which will reflect the negativity back to the source of it, *with love*. That is important. You don't want to incur any karma. The recipient will soon stop sending you bad vibes. This may have been unintentional on their part anyway; they just had strong feelings which were transmitted to you.

Another thing which you might like to try if you know who is causing you the trouble, is to write their name on a piece of paper and put it into a cup of black coffee and freeze it. If you don't feel happy about having that energy in your freezer, you could then bury the frozen coffee in the earth and it will be transmuted. Mother Earth doesn't recognise 'good energy' or 'negative energy' it is all just energy to be utilised.

Qi Gong

Pronounced, *Chee* Gong, this is very popular form of exercise in the East and the popularity is spreading worldwide. Qi Gong is an ancient health giving exercise which is part of Traditional Chinese Medicine, (TCM) and dates back around 5000 years. It is comprised of both moving and passive or meditational exercises which are designed to stimulate the body's energy or Qi system. Regular practice promotes good general health and a peaceful mind.

I was privileged to attend classes in *Da Yan Qi Gong* . This is a particularly beautiful form of Qi Gong as it imitates the movements of a Wild Goose (*Da Yan* in Chinese). It stimulates the immune system and balances the body through 70 sets of postures.

Readings

Readings can come under the headings of Tarot, Palmistry, Psychometry, Numerology, Runes and much more. The person giving the 'reading' often uses a tool such as cards to lead them into a session where they use their psychic skills to tune into the energy field of their client and they can then 'read' various things from their past and present. Any foretelling of future events is always open as we live on a free-will planet and are able to consciously create and change our plans. Nothing need be set in stone, as it were. Some people channel information from Ascended Masters, Angels and guides, while others are mediums who bring forward evidence of continuing life after physical death from family members and friends who have passed on. Yet others use purely their psychic and intuitive skills to give information to their clients.

You can give yourself a reading from various packs of cards readily available nowadays. This can be very helpful at times of indecision or great change in your life. Don't, however, become reliant on another person who 'tells you what to do' as this will stifle your own inherent intuition and inner guidance. If in doubt, follow what your heart tells you. You will just *feel* whether or not something is right for you.

Reincarnation

Dictionary ~ the belief that on the death of the body the soul transmigrates to or is born again in another body.

We are all in the process of evolving and some have lived many, many, lives here on Earth and possibly on other planets, even in other universes. Think about a butterfly - it starts off as an egg, then a caterpillar then pupae and finally becomes a beautiful butterfly.

We are similar in that we have had to go through many stages of life to reach the point where we are now. We will have been both male and female, warrior and peacemaker, rich and poor, leader and servant, murderer and the murdered, mother, father, sister, brother, daughter, son and so on.

Over eons, we have accumulated experiences and wisdom, and in this lifetime, we have come to 'Earth School' to experience something in particular. Look back over your life and see if there are repeating situations. This will give you some clues as to what your soul wishes to experience. You will keep attracting people and circumstances into your life until you have learnt the lesson about forgiveness or unconditional love or whatever it was that you contracted to learn before you incarnated. Do you keep making the wrong choice of partner? Is betrayal a recurring pattern in your life? Is there someone (or many people) you feel unable to forgive? You will continue to be given opportunities to change and make a better choice. There is always another chance. Don't beat yourself up if you realise that you were being tested and you reacted unwisely when someone pressed your buttons. You didn't fail. You are human; you are not expected to be perfect. There will be another opportunity along soon! When the timing is appropriate, someone will activate a response in you.

Apparently, in between lives, we sometimes do a quick turnaround and immediately reincarnate, and at other times, we spend a while learning in the Halls of Wisdom. We choose what we need to experience in the next lifetime, and other dear souls agree to be the ones to help us with our lessons. The people who may have been 'bad' to us in this life are really our teachers, and they really love us very much at a soul level.

We choose our parents and therefore where we will be born, our skin colour and the type of civilisation we are entering. Think about this, and ask yourself what you have learned from having your particular parents. Have circumstances made you more independent? Were your talents encouraged or stifled? Were you surrounded by love or did you choose a dysfunctional family? We choose specific events that we need to experience and people that we want to have as partners and friends. Some things are 'set in stone' and must be experienced. The rest of our life unfolds depending upon our choices. There is no right or wrong – just the consequences of our choices. It is the planet of free will - Earth School.

I found that this gave me quite a different perspective on events, and made it much easier to forgive the people who I perceived as having hurt me. I can no longer be a victim. I must take responsibility for everything that happens in my life. After all, I planned much of it before I came in, and I am so grateful to all of the many people who have come into my life to help me learn a lesson or have a particular experience.

I look forward to the day when I have experienced all that I need to and can live completely in unconditional love. I will not need to return here again for any more human experiences but will be able to go Home and be at one with God.

Sacred Space

Having a protected sacred space in your home or work room is vital if you are involved in healing work of any kind. It ensures that both your client and yourself are safe at all times and that only extremely high vibrational energies can enter the area. It will provide a beautiful, serene environment in which to do meditation or yoga as well.

Making protected sacred space is a three-fold thing. First of all, you must clean the area. Remember that where there is physical dirt there is also psychic dirt. So, that means dusting and vacuuming or whatever is necessary. Secondly, clear the area of negative or stuck energy by whatever means you choose. You may like to clap out the corners with your hands until the sound is clear, or drum or ring a bell, or perhaps draw symbols into the room. Reading a book on space clearing will give you helpful ideas. It is a good idea to light a candle and perhaps burn some incense or essential oils.

Next, *create* your sacred space by physically walking around the room in an anti-clockwise direction at least three times, holding either a candle, or incense or just your strong intention along with energy if you are an energy worker. You might also like to invite in angels or ascended masters to work with you.

Well done, you have now created a protected, sacred space in which to work.

I add on the following words nowadays – "I place filters over the doors and windows, the chimneys, cat flap, ventilators and any cracks, so that only that which works *totally* for the Light may enter, and anything else is trapped and instantly transmuted out into the universe, with love."

You may feel that this is overdoing it a bit, but as I work from home, I decided that there was little point in having a cleared protected space in my treatment room, if people were coming into my house with all sorts of 'stuff' in their energy field which was being dumped in my hallway or elsewhere! I imagine that they are being 'sieved' as they enter my front door now, so only love and light enters my home.

Scrying

Dictionary ~ *to divine, especially by crystal gazing.*

Those who can look into crystal balls and can foretell events or see objects connected with a person's life are scrying. Scrying can also be done with a bowl of water or by gazing into a still pool, or a mirror or clouds, or smoke. Try it for yourself. It is just a tool for giving a reading to someone in much the same way as another person might use tarot cards or runes or coloured ribbons. It is a helper for your psychic abilities. Just say what you see, and that makes way for the next lot of information to come through.

Shamanism

Dictionary ~ *the religion of certain peoples, based on the belief that the world is pervaded by good and evil spirits who can be influenced or controlled only by the shamans.*

In ancient times, our ancestors lived with great understanding of nature and the elements. Their lives often depended upon the seasons, the availability of water and the use of fire. In many tribes, there was no distinction between the care of the physical body (medicine) and the spiritual body (religion). The shaman cared for the mind, the body and the spirit.

The word 'shaman' comes from the ancient language of the Tungus, a tribe from North-Central Asia, and came into use via the Russian language and derives from the verb 'sa', which means, 'to know'. However the term shaman is generally applied to healers, seers, medicine and holy men in many different cultures throughout the world today.

Many shamans use a drum as a tool to help you fall into an alpha state of consciousness where you can then go on a meditational journey into the underworld to retrieve parts of your soul which may have been lost, or to face your shadow aspects and acknowledge and release them. Many shamans are accredited with being able to control the weather, interpret dreams, astral travel and meet with spirits in the upper or lower worlds.

The Native American traditions are very shamanic, involving drumming, chanting, dancing, working with smoke, feathers and rattles. Similar traditions are regularly followed in Siberia, South America, Africa and Australia by the indigenous races.

Shamanism can be traced back 50,000 years to the Stone Age and is still very much alive today.

Shapeshifting

Shapeshifting is something which the shamanic races are attributed as being able to do. It is the ability to be able to merge from one reality into another; to be able to move into and become a tree, or a rock or an animal. It has been suggested that perhaps that is an explanation as to what happened to the Mayans who disappeared without trace – they just shape-shifted into another dimension!

The advanced races such as the ancient Egyptians, Atlanteans, the Mayans, even the Aztecs and Incas probably trained in the art of shapeshifting. Try it yourself. When you are alone and able to be still beside a tree, for example, lean against the tree and ask to feel its energy. You may be privileged to be allowed to merge your energy field with the tree's and may experience 'being the tree'. You may feel the sap as it flows upwards from the roots bringing nourishment to the extremities. The tree may impart some knowledge or wisdom to you or you may be aware of a particular colour or emotion. With practice, you may eventually be able to shape shift into a tree.

Over the next few years as the veils between the different dimensions fade and we become more aware of the other realities surrounding us, we may find that we are able to shift into and out of these other worlds at will.

On a lighter note, when walking in the hills or on rough, stony terrain, say to yourself, 'I'm sure-footed as a mountain goat' and you will find that you will be less likely to fall. When swimming, say, 'I can swim like a fish' and you will glide lightly through the water. (Remember, energy follows thought).

Sound healing

Dictionary ~ Sound - *the sensations produced by a periodic disturbance in the organs of hearing. To resonate with a certain quality or intensity.*

Sound healing can take many forms. Some healers channel sounds, singing and other languages during a session. There are teachers who work with the voice and teach methods of chanting, singing and speaking which stretch the pupil's capacity to communicate as well as giving healing on all levels.

Drumming is another very powerful method of sound healing and this is utilised by the Shamanic traditions and also by modern sound healers. The hypnotic sound of a drumbeat can quickly put you into a meditational state and then you may be led through a guided visualisation called a drum journey.

The use of singing bowls, either quartz or brass, is also extremely effective as the vibrations can be felt throughout the body. A shaped stick-like tool, is used to stroke around the rim of the singing bowl until it starts to sound its note. If it is a large quartz bowl, the sound is magnificent, and travels through the floor and resounds around the room; wonderful for shaking out any negativity when space clearing. Singing bowls are available which sound any note of the scale.

Some practitioners work with tuning forks. They can be used to balance the chakras and subtle bodies. This is becoming popular nowadays. Each of us resonates with a particular note and it can be helpful for you to discover which is *your* note.

I channel sound through the **Hathors** (see the chapter of that title).

Spirit

Dictionary ~ *the force or principal of life that animates the body of living things.*

We don't *have* a spirit, we *are* Spirit. We are amazing beings of light and energy who have been around for probably eons, and when we decide to incarnate on Earth, to have particular experiences, we take on a physical appearance. The body we have is no more than a 'hired car' which we've chosen for this journey (*see the chapter on* Auras).

We are immortal, everlasting, Divine and constantly evolving and transforming until we can one day return to our spiritual home with our Creator God, Source, All That Is or whatever name is more familiar to you.

Starseeds

'Starseeds' are highly evolved beings from other planets, galaxies or star systems, who have come to help on planet Earth at this time. They will have incarnated in the same way as other humans with the same 'amnesia' about their origins, but they will be given a wake-up call at a specific time in their lives to alert them to their calling. They will not be fazed with the idea of aliens, intergalactic travel, starships etc. That will all appear to be logical. They will probably have little interest in religion, politics or economics preferring to study esoteric matters. They may have an interest in healing, writing and other creative work. Some may feel isolated and different from others which may lead to depression as they feel misunderstood. They may find it hard to live in the heavy third dimension but as their life unfolds and they release their fear based patterns and start to live through love, this will impact on everyone around them and gradually affect the collective consciousness in a positive way.

Do you feel that you may have come from the stars? Do you have an interest in UFO's, ET's, feel that you *have* to be of service to humanity in some way, are spiritually awakened and probably going through some turmoil in your life? Well, there is no need to be afraid. There are thousands of you out there in the world. You are probably a starseed and are just answering your call. Although you may not remember, you agreed to come to the aid of Earth at this time and your mission is of love and service. Thank you for that.

There are a number of websites and books which you will find helpful.

Talisman

Dictionary ~ *a stone or other small object, usually inscribed or carved; believed to protect the wearer from evil influences. Anything thought to have magical or protective powers.*

A talisman is another name for an amulet, sometimes believed to have mystical powers. When I was young, it was very common for people to wear a St. Christopher medallion around their neck for protection, particularly when travelling. Some people had a lucky rabbit's foot (not so lucky for the rabbit!) or a four leafed clover. The cross or crucifix is of course still very popular.

Most people if questioned will admit to having a particular stone, crystal, small object or medallion which they consider to be lucky or protective. As crystals or gemstones tend to absorb negativity and each has its own particular energy to offer us, they are very popular nowadays and can be worn as any form of jewellery or just carried in a pocket.

From the ankh and scarab of Egypt to the charm bracelet of the western world, to the turquoise and silver necklaces of the Native Americans, talismans continue to be a part of our lives.

Telekinesis

Dictionary ~ *the movement of a body caused by thought or willpower without the application of a physical force.*

The causing of an object to move by means of psychic energy or mind power has been practised for centuries. Telekinesis or Psychokinesis as it is also known can appear as a gift, particularly in teenagers. Poltergeist activity, when objects are moved or fly around the room, is often put down to the unconscious behaviour of a child going through puberty.

As with all psychic phenomena, there is a lot of disagreement as to validity and there is still controversy within the sciences and even parapsychology schools as to the existence of telekinesis.

The person who most people associate with this use of energy is Uri Geller, famous for his spoon bending and other fascinating feats.

Totem

Dictionary ~ *an object, animal, plant etc. symbolising a clan, family etc., often having ritual associations.*

The Native American Indians are probably most associated with totems. They have totem animals and myths which have been handed down through the generations to the present day. Totem poles are carved with animals, birds and lizards and spiritually represent the tribe or clan. Totem poles are not confined to America however; there are totems in Sanxingdui in China and also in Zimbabwe in use by the Shona people.

Animal totems can be seen as archetypes that can be tapped into by our electromagnetic energy fields depending upon our needs at the time. The animal will express the qualities from which we can learn. This is not a worshipping of the animal, rather an honouring and respect for nature of which we are all a part.

Unconditional Love

Dictionary ~ Unconditional – *without limitations.*

The dictionary definition says it all. In simple terms, to love someone unconditionally means to have no expectations. To simply accept them the way they are without judgement. It has nothing to do with romantic love. It is simply acceptance.

When we can love everyone unconditionally, we will have achieved what we came here to do.

Uncording

Whenever we have a relationship with someone, no matter how fleeting, we form cords in the etheric which are attached at various parts of the body. By the time we are adult, we therefore have a number of cords attaching us to numerous people from parents and siblings and friends, to teachers, workmates, lovers and so on.

Some cords are necessary, such as the ones between parents and children under sixteen. However, in our culture, there is no ceremony for cutting the ties. In other parts of the world, native ceremonies declare that a boy has now become a man, or a girl has now become a woman, but no such ceremony exists here. An 18th or 21st birthday party is not quite the same thing. This means that parents keep on feeling responsible for their offspring no matter what their age! The offspring also feel the influence of the parent and this can cause lots of aggravation.

As a result, we go through life with unnecessary cords attaching us to many people, some who may have passed on. We can be affected by this, as the person attached to us can influence our thoughts or behaviour in the same way as we may have been affected by them in the past as a child, for example. Have you ever planned to do something, when you've heard in the back of your mind, "You won't be able to do that" or "You'll never amount to anything" or something similar? Was it what a parent perhaps said to you years ago? It could be that because you still have cords of attachment, they are still able to influence you and 'press your buttons'.

It is wise to take yourself through an uncording procedure and cut any unnecessary attachments to all the people in your life, beginning with the ones closest to you. It doesn't mean that you are severing your connection with them (unless you intend that). Quite the opposite, you will find that you will have a stronger, more positive relationship as you are both able to stand in your own power.

There are many ways of doing this, but the intention is everything. If someone can lead you through it, all to the good, but otherwise just do this for yourself. Begin by sitting or lying in a comfortable position in a quiet room where you will not be distracted. Take a few deep breaths to relax your body and still your mind. Visualise the person you wish to uncord from standing before you. (If for any reason you are afraid of them, if you've been a victim of abuse for example, put a circle of light around their feet and a circle of light around your own feet, and you are protected).

Next, 'look' up and down them and see, feel or just know, where there are cords of attachment. Sometimes the cords are as thick as telegraph poles and sometimes as thin as spaghetti. You may even feel that the person is holding your feet or has a net over you or something similar. They may be connected via the chakras. Just go with whatever comes into your mind. When you have established where the cords or whatever are, then you can either cut or pull them out yourself by visualising that, or you can call upon the Archangel Michael.

Michael will cut all unnecessary attachments in an instant with his sword. You may be aware of the cut ends dissolving in gold light back into you and the other person. Now walk with the person into a beautiful 'waterfall of light' which will wash over you both and completely remove any negativity placed upon you.

When you feel ready, walk out of the light, hand in hand and smiling. Allow their image to gently disappear. Repeat the procedure with another person on your list. You will have to do this over a period of time until all attachments are removed. Be aware that they start to grow again immediately with our loved ones, so it is advisable to do an 'uncording' at least annually to keep yourself free of unwanted influence.

If you prefer to cut the cords by yourself without angelic help, then imagine that you are in a beautiful garden and use all of your senses as you walk through it, hearing the birds and insects, smelling the flowers, seeing the sky and the surroundings etc. Make your way to a summer house and sit down on a bench there. The person from whom you wish to uncord will come to sit on a bench opposite. Observe where there are attachments, as before, then look down at your hands and there will be some implement there to enable you to cut the cords. Do each cord one at a time until you are both free. When you've finished, walk back through the garden and bring yourself back to your room and ground yourself. Have some water and walk around. Repeat the procedure with as many people as you feel appropriate at each session.

Sometimes you may feel that you want to say something to the person concerned. You may want to ask their forgiveness or ask why they did what they did. This is particularly the case when you are attached to someone who has made their transition, but is still influencing you from 'beyond the grave'. Say whatever you feel, and remember that they will now be able to answer you from a higher perspective and so will clear up misunderstandings or at least give you some indication as to the reasons for their actions in the past.

You will always benefit from uncording from all unnecessary attachments and be able to stand in your own power and speak your own truth.

The Violet Flame

The Violet Flame or Violet Fire is a gift to humanity from our Father Mother God. It is a spiritual energy which can heal emotional and physical problems and can be utilised by everyone. The Violet Flame comes from the Violet Ray which has the qualities of mercy, forgiveness, freedom and transmutation. The colour violet has long been associated with spirituality and has the highest frequency in the visible spectrum.

It is the masculine sapphire blue flame of Divine Will, Power and Authority of our Father God and the feminine crystalline pink flame of Transfiguring Divine Love, Adoration and Reverence for Life. Transmutation means to change, alter appearance or nature; (think of a caterpillar turning into a butterfly). The Violet Flame can change negative energy into positive energy, darkness into light.

It was given to us for our use early in the twentieth century by Saint Germain, an Ascended Master. The Violet Flame has the alchemical ability to transform anxiety into peace, and fear into courage and love. It is a tool to help raise our frequency and conscious awareness, release karma and speed up our spiritual growth.

All we have to do to take advantage of this wonderful gift is to invoke it through our mighty I AM Presence. We need to ask for it in order to receive.

Surround yourself with protection beforehand then say something along the lines of the following: "**I call forth my mighty I Am Presence and through Divine Grace and Light, I now invoke the Violet Flame to transmute the energies in and around [my body, place of work, the planet, person's name etc] and to transform them into Light.**
So be it. And so it is."

Remember to call on your I Am Presence and the exact wording is not as important as the **intention.** Visualise the colour violet swirling around the focus of your intention if you can.

The Violet Flame can transmute anything we want to heal in ourselves, thereby healing the planet. All we have to do is invoke the Violet Flame through our I Am Presence to transform anything in our lives which does not reflect the Divine. Persevere as this **does** work.

Recommended reading – *Are You a Master of Light?* by Louise Hopkinson and Jane White

Visualisation

Dictionary ~ to *form a mental image of something not at that moment visible.*

A visualisation can be a form of meditation which is very powerful and can give healing at a deep level. It can also be used to access incidents in the past where they can be viewed as though on a screen, making it more comfortable for the person involved to cope with and to release the negativity surrounding the incident.

There are many tapes and CD's available with guided visualisations and many included in books. It is always easier to access a deep state of relaxation if someone else is either reading the instructions to you or you are listening to a recording. Take sufficient time to relax all your muscles and slow down your breathing. Just simply 'watching' your breath go in....and out....in...and out... can be a good way to meditate. In your mind, take yourself off to someplace that you love. It could be a seashore, a forest, a mountainside, a garden or someplace else. Just experiencing the surroundings with all of your senses in turn is a wonderfully relaxing form of visualisation (see chapter on *Meditation).*

Walk-in

Let me try to explain this one. In certain circumstances, if someone was ready to die, the spirit of another being who wanted to come into the earth plane as an adult could make a contract with the first person. The first person's spirit leaves, and the new one takes over the physical body and all of the memories. This usually happens when someone is either very ill, is in a coma, has had a nervous breakdown or something similar. When they recover, they feel quite different (which of course, they are) and friends and family may notice that they have changed in some way. The process can take a long time, or it can happen very quickly. Usually the incoming being has important spiritual work to do and that is why there isn't time for them to be born and grow up. They may be able to integrate with the family and friends in the same way as the original being, but sometimes the changes are too great, and separations occur from husbands/partners and offspring.

If the memories are not constantly revitalised and close contact kept with family and friends, the 'new' person can easily drift away from relationships.

There is another explanation for an apparent walk-in situation. It may not necessarily be a 'new' spirit entering the body, it could be that the person in question has completed their contract for this lifetime and their Higher Self has allowed them to make a shift in evolution and they are elevated to another dimension of being in this lifetime. They literally cast off the old and put on the new. It is a bit like the transformation of a butterfly. They can then do further work which ordinarily would have taken another lifetime. They *feel* different, and just like the other type of walk-in, they can often pinpoint the exact day when it happened.

Water

Dictionary ~ a *clear, colourless, tasteless, odourless liquid that is essential for plant and animal life and constitutes, in impure form, rain, oceans, rivers, lakes etc.*

Since the beginning of time, it has been essential for all living creatures to have a continual supply of water for survival. Our human bodies are made up of approximately 70% water which needs to be renewed daily. In many of us, the desire to drink has been dulled, and we only drink when really thirsty. Even then, the array of beverages available such as tea, coffee, soft drinks, fruit juices and of course, alchohol, means that some people never drink plain water. Although there is some water in all beverages, some of them are dehydrating, and others downright toxic. Many people are therefore extremely dehydrated and that explains many of the pains and illnesses appearing today.

The brain takes 20% of available water from your body for it to work, so it is easy to see how your muscles and tissue are starved of water if you do not replace this with copious drinks of plain water throughout the day. Much of the constipation, digestive problems and arthritis in today's civilisation could be alleviated by simply drinking water.

I recommend that you read Dr. F. Batmanghelidj's book, 'Your Body's Many Cries for Water'.

Most people require about 2 litres of water per day; more if you do physical work or in hot weather. If you are a therapist or energy worker, you *must* drink loads of water and may need more than 2 litres. Dowse to find out your personal requirements.

Water has long been the symbol for our emotions. Just as the moon affects the tides, so do our emotions ebb and flow. We talk about feeling 'all at sea' or 'feeling adrift' when going through a difficult time. The composition of our blood is very similar to sea water. Our tears are salt water.

As well as being necessary just to keep us alive, water connects us with the rest of the planet. Each drop of water in each puddle, stream, river and ocean can be affected by our thoughts and intentions. Dr. Masaru Emoto's work, through analysing water crystals, has brought the knowledge to the world that the composition of water can be altered by our thoughts. He has shown by clear photographic evidence that water which has been subjected to words such as, *hate, war, anger* will not form into complete crystals when frozen. If the water has words like, *peace, love and gratitude,* placed beside it, the crystals formed will be perfect, like beautiful crystal snowflakes. I thoroughly recommend Dr. Emoto's book, *The Messages from Water.*

We can all begin to make a difference to our planet by blessing the water which we drink and use for washing and cooking each day. Place a label with *love and gratitude* on your water jug or kettle.

You can buy coasters which have positive words printed on them specifically for placing under cups and jugs etc. or you could simply make your own. Just the simple act of holding a cup of water in your hands and blessing it and then pouring it into the ground, can help heal the earth. Don't think that you can't possibly do anything as you are too small. Remember, *energy follows thought*, and that is very powerful. Sending love to the planet each day will soon make a huge difference. We are not working alone. Remember that there are other agencies at work here. Angels, elementals, ascended masters, all willing us to strive to save our planet. We are all ONE.

Wicca

Dictionary ~ the *cult or practice of witchcraft.*

Wicca is a way of life, working closely with nature and with a strong belief in God and Goddess. There are many ceremonies and rituals and celebration of Goddess, some honouring the Moon. Sacred space is created in the form of the magic circle and regular blessings are made.

Wicca dates back to pre-Christian pagan times and combines magick and mysticism with spirituality. It is not strictly true to say that it is the same as witchcraft. All Wiccans are Witches but not all Witches are Wiccan. Witches don't necessarily accept God/Goddess as their deity. To be a Wiccan it is necessary to be accepted by a coven for training, then after time, be initiated and follow the life, gaining experience in the practical, spiritual and mystical tradition and thoroughly integrating the ethics into your everyday life.

X

There is no word beginning with X that I can think of which comes up in a spiritual sense.

In mathematics, x commonly represents an unknown variable. In genetics, x denotes the x chromosome.

In the game noughts and crosses, it represents a cross. However, probably one of the most common ways that people use an X is to write the word, Xmas. This is one of my pet hates! **Don't keep the Christ out of Christmas!** Another common and much nicer form of x is when you put it at the end of a letter to represent a kiss.

Yantra

The root of the word, Yantra, is to *sustain*. The yantra is an abstract geometrical design in the form of a mandala, used as a tool for meditation and increased awareness. It refers to Devi or Goddess in her geometrical form.

The most popular yantra is Sri Yantra shown below.

This can be etched in copper and worn as a medallion or viewed as a picture. There are numerous books on the subject and further information on the internet.

155

Yoga

Dictionary ~ A *Hindu system of philosophy aiming at the mystical union of the self with the Supreme Being in a state of complete awareness and tranquillity through certain physical and mental exercises and postures.*

Yoga originated in India, strongly connected with Hinduism, where it is part of a group of spiritual practices, also a spiritual tradition thought to bring enlightenment. In the West, Hatha yoga with its *asanas* or postures is the most popular form of yoga and many people regularly attend classes and have daily routines for exercise and to help them to remain calm and centred.

Modern yoga draws on the ancient spiritual traditions of eastern religion and may include instruction in the moral and ethical principles and spiritual philosophy, breathing exercises, the chanting of mantras, postures to encourage flexibility and fitness and meditation to still the mind.

It is important to find a teacher (yogi) with whom you feel comfortable, who will encourage you to practise daily, thereby improving your health: physically, emotionally and mentally, and giving a heightened sense of well-being.

Yoga can be a way of increasing spiritual awareness, without necessarily having a Hindu connection, and greater compassion and unconditional love can result. Realisation of the non-duality of the universe and no-separation may be the ultimate reward when the limiting ego is 'enlightened'.

Zen

Dictionary ~ *a Japanese school of 12th Century Chinese origin, teaching that contemplation of one's essential nature to the exclusion of all else is the only way of achieving pure enlightenment.*

Chan was a tradition started in the first century in China when Buddhism arrived from India. It then travelled to Japan, where it became known as Zen. Zen Buddhism is a form of *Mahayana Buddhism* and is a way of life, not just a state of consciousness. DT Susuki wrote "the aspects of this life are: a life of humility, a life of labour, a life of service, a life of prayer and gratitude and a life of meditation."

The core practice of Zen is a sitting meditation called, Zazen. This involves sitting, perhaps in the lotus position for example, and concentrating on posture and the breath. The practice may be for only five minutes daily at first, while monks may have several periods of zazen lasting for thirty to forty minutes each.

You may have seen a Japanese Rock Garden or Zen Garden. This consists of rocks, sand and gravel and there may be a few grasses but plants are not essential. The sand represents the sea and is raked to simulate ripples in the water. The rocks or pebbles can represent islands or mountains. Sometimes, but not always, the garden is meant to be viewed from one particular perspective.

At the Ryoanji Temple in Kyoto, Japan, a rock garden has been arranged where 15 rocks have been strategically placed so that only 14 can be seen from any point in the garden at any time. Legend has it that only when someone becomes spiritually enlightened through the practice of deep Zen meditation can the invisible 15th stone be seen in the mind's eye.

Much of Zen practice has to do with living in the present moment.

'*Whatever people do, whether they remain in the world as artisans, merchants, or officers of the government, let them put their whole heart into the task; let them be diligent and energetic. And if, like the lotus flower, which grows out of muddy water but remains untouched by the mud, they engage in life without cherishing envy or hatred; if they live in the world not a life of self but a life of truth, then surely joy, peace and bliss will dwell in their minds.*'

Buddhacarita

Printed in the United Kingdom
by Lightning Source UK Ltd.
116908UKS00001B/88-135